CHAOS OR PEACE
IN THE CASTLE — IN THE PALACE

STRAIGHTEN YOUR CROWN ✤ CAPTURE HIS HEART
DISCOVER YOUR HAPPILY EVER AFTER

2nd Edition

DAN & LYDIA WHITE

Published by Author Academy Elite
PO Box 43, Powell, OH 43065
www.AuthorAcademyElite.com

Identifiers:

LCCN: 2020908194
ISBN: 978-1-64746-263-5 (paperback)
ISBN: 978-1-64746-264-2 (hardback)
ISBN: 978-1-64746-265-9 (ebook)

Available in paperback, hardback, e-book, and audiobook

All Scripture quotations, unless otherwise indicated, are taken from the Holy Bible, New International Version®, NIV®. Copyright © 1973, 1978, 1984 by Biblica, Inc.™ Used by permission of Zondervan. All rights reserved worldwide.

See Appendix B for details and copyright information on additional scripture translations used.

Any Internet addresses (websites, blogs, etc.) and telephone numbers printed in this book are offered as a resource. They are not intended in any way to be or imply an endorsement by Author Academy Elite, nor does Author Academy Elite vouch for the content of these sites and numbers for the life of this book.

TABLE OF CONTENTS

INTRODUCTION

Dan and I are so excited you've chosen to join us as we explore new ideas about love and marriage in the pages of this book! As a woman, I believe there's something in us all that longs to live in a perfect world and be the queen of our palace not just for a day, but for a lifetime. Wouldn't you love to stand arm in arm with your dashing knight in shining armor, seeing him as a brave warrior and a noble leader? I think if we're honest we can all admit this fantasy is not too far from the truth of our dreams, despite the fact it might seem a little farfetched.

As we've encountered countless love stories in the movies we've watched and the books we've read, clues are everywhere suggesting that the wish for a fanciful fairy tale with a kingdom, a palace, and a happy ending is at the core of our human DNA. Storylines throughout history from ancient fables to modern-day fairy tales are all rooted in this idea. From Disney films to thrilling superhero movies, the evidence is even more compelling as plots unfold revealing the same underlying theme. The hero rescues the damsel in distress, squashes the villain, and saves the day! Writers, both male and female, continue to write their stories with compelling characters telling the same saga in a new way over and over again. For that reason, I wanted my husband and I to write this book together. I needed his masculine perspective. For clarity, even though we both contributed to the book, I will be sharing from my heart woman to woman.

How do men view their role in this heroic picture of *happily ever after*? Most of them probably have a much simpler dream than their female counterparts. Nonetheless, many are still filled with some fantastic expectations for themselves and their future. As boys, they often dream of being someone's hero. As Dan and I watched our sons growing up, they always play the valiant warrior who defeats the *bad guy*. That's why men love action packed films as adults. They often relate to and even imagine themselves like the heroes they admire in the movies they watch. Deep in a man's heart he longs to go out and conquer the world in his career, bring home the prize from the hunt, and lay in bed at night with the damsel of his dreams.

Even though these ideas are based on fairytales, realistically from the time you and I are little girls the idea of *Happily Ever After* captures our imagination and fascinates our hearts. It creates a desire in us for the fantasy to become our story. Most women will agree they long for an enchanted life that will last into the *ever after* while questioning if it can be a reality, especially with today's statistics of broken relationships. The truth is *Ever After* is not enough when it stands alone unless the love story has *Happily* at the beginning.

As far as happiness goes, some couples go into marriage realistically knowing it won't be that easy. Others walk down the aisle with blinders on, having no idea what it will take to live a life close to their own version of happiness. Some unrealistically believe in the automatic fairytale ending before they ever say "I do", while many modern-day couples don't believe in the wedding nuptials at all. Instead, they pack up their bags and their toothbrush and move in, seeking a less complicated route without a solid commitment. That way, if it doesn't work out, they can move out and just move on.

Realistically, there are no manuals given out once you've moved in together or cut the cake and tossed the bouquet. For that reason, making love last a lifetime can seem overwhelming. That's why Dan and I have written this book for women and the companion book for men called, *Marriage Warrior*. We believe they can change the trajectory of your relationship. We know from experience it's never too late to start building or remodeling the castle you've got into the palace you desire. As you take this journey through history with us, you'll learn things you've never heard before. As we began to research and write, we discovered insights about marriage that completely transformed our lives. It gave us the opportunity for a happier, healthier life together than ever before. This information can do the same for you. It will empower you to begin a new chapter in your love story. We know you can find real freedom in the person you were created to be so you and your mate can find a love for each other as never before. You are destined to become the queen of your palace. You *can* straighten your crown, capture his heart, and discover your happily ever after!

FOUNDATIONS

Chapter 1

WILL YOU BUILD A CASTLE OR A PALACE?

When you saw the title of this book you may have asked yourself, "What's the difference between a castle and a palace?" Most people think they're the same thing, but according to historical references, a castle was built for war and a palace was a refuge of peace. Castles were surrounded by moats and fortified for battle. Palaces had no fortification and could be built anywhere because the nobles who owned them went there for a little royal rest and relaxation. I don't know about you, but I prefer the peaceful palace over the war-torn castle any day.

Have you looked around lately? There's a battle going on around us and it is pushing us all into the *chaotic castle* lifestyle. Our marriages are in trouble, and there seems to be no end in sight to the mess we've created. With the confusion that surrounds us, we're living with chaos in our castles surrounded by a moat of, well… *you know what*. I mean that literally, and it's up to us to figure out how to turn the tide. Why? Because if we don't, we'll lose sight of the palace and our children will have no blueprint to follow to build their future.

From the beginning of time, marriage was established as the foundation for all human family relationships. That means if the foundation for marriage crumbles, the rest of our relationships will come tumbling down just like Jill following Jack down the hill after he fell down and broke his royal crown.

WHAT IS THE PURPOSE OF A MOAT?

In medieval times, a moat was a body of water completely surrounding a castle. They were a form of protection serving as fortification to help keep an enemy from seizing access to the kingdom and destroying the royal family that lived inside. Many of the moats surrounding early castles also served as sewage systems. They were septic tanks of sorts, and they helped discourage invading chaos on a whole new level.

Today unlike the moats of the past, the moats that are surrounding us aren't protecting us at all. In fact, they're getting so full of the issues in our cultural war they're threatening to overflow into our homes and destroy everything that matters. Trust me when I speak from personal experience regarding overflowing moats. A few years ago, as all thirty-three family members gathered to celebrate Christmas at my husband's parents; suddenly chaos invaded our gathering. The septic tank backed up and overflowed into the basement, and what started out as a holiday soon turned into a swashbuckling mess on the poop deck with buckets, mops, and all! Believe me when I say, "It's not a pretty sight to have a moat flowing through your home!"

Through the years, there have been a few times I was sure Dan and I needed a life raft to ride the tide of sewage threatening to overtake our palace. The three things we had going for us was our commitment to the promises we made on our wedding day, the covenant they represented, and sheer determination not to ever give up. Before we even said "I do" we decided that the *D-word* would never be allowed in our conversations or confrontations. As you may have guessed, the *D-word* stands for "Divorce" but a better way to think of it is *the Door*. We both agreed before our wedding day that if we believed in the possibility of an *exit* door, we'd be tempted to put our hand on the knob and walk-out when things got tough. Today, with the high number of couples choosing to live together versus getting married, many are living with an *exit* door in their lives, and they don't even know it. The truth is, whether married or not, an *exit* door is not just any door, it's a *trapdoor* that leads to complete chaos in the castle instead of peace in the palace.

WHERE DOES THE TRAP DOOR LEAD?

Back in the days of castles, kings, and queens, the doors were not so easy to open. They weren't small, simple doors giving nobles easy access to come and go as they pleased. They were like the castle doors seen in the movies, exceptionally large and extremely heavy. They served as protection, requiring multiple people to raise and lower the doors operating on a dangerous pulley system. These doors made lots of noise where no one could easily sneak in or out. Maybe that's why the divorce rate was so low back then. Today no one really notices or makes any noise when divorce happens. Marriage has become a revolving door, light weight and easy to open. Unfortunately, in most marriages, there is more than one door to choose from and walk through. Some people leave their marriage through the door called *career* while others leave through the doors of *financial strain or gain* or *irreconcilable differences*. Then there are those who run because the grass looks a whole lot greener *over there*.

To be honest, there have been a few times in our thirty plus years of marriage I wished for a trapdoor like those you see at a magic show. You know the door inside the cabinet where the beautiful female assistant gets to step through and disappear. The few times I've wanted to vanish, it was because something tough was happening and I wanted out. Then suddenly I would snap into reality and remember there was no way out. I had made a commitment a long time ago to myself and my husband that there would never be an *exit door* in this relationship. I was dedicated to that promise, and that commitment really mattered to me.

WHY DO PEOPLE CHOOSE TO LEAVE THROUGH THE TRAP DOOR?

I remember watching a wild and crazy game show as a child called *Let's Make a Deal* with a host named Monty Hall. The show was so popular that recently it's made a modern-day comeback. The main idea behind the show was the trades and negotiations between the host and audience members who were trying to take home the biggest and best prize. The top three winners at the end of the show got to try for the *bigger deal*. At that point they could choose to keep the loot they had or give it up and trade it in for "Door # 1, Door # 2, or Door # 3!" There was always the possibility behind the door of their choice of getting a grander prize. The probability of getting something they didn't bargain for was even greater. The hook was the risk and intrigue of what *could be*. Comical chaos set in when contestants won prizes that they didn't count on like a two-hundred-pound pig, a stubborn donkey, or maybe even a pot of dung instead of a pot of gold.

If we're truthful, most of us have considered choosing a different door at some point. Just like the contestants on *Let's Make a Deal*, it's in our human nature to be captivated by the idea of something better waiting on the other side. I experienced this phenomenon shopping for my wedding dress. The first bridal boutique my mom and I entered had the dress I'd dreamed of inside my head, and I immediately tried it on. It was the color I wanted, the design I'd imagined, and it fit beautifully. It would have been the fastest wedding dress purchase in history. However, I thought the next best dress might be waiting in the next store through the next door. This possibility took us into boutique after boutique, trying on dress after dress, for the next six hours. By the end of the day every dress looked the same, and we were exhausted. I couldn't remember what I liked, or which store I saw what dress in. Our heads were both spinning. As mom and I sat quietly in the car gathering our thoughts, I suddenly had an epiphany. It was the first dress I tried on! I panicked, realizing it could be gone because it was on sale. We rushed back to the original store. Miraculously, it was still hanging on the rack. Needless to say, I said "YES" to the dress! As I reflected, I realized our day could have been much more fun and carefree had I not fallen for the possibility of what might be behind door #1, door #2, or door #3. This lesson is applicable not only to shopping but to our marriage as well.

Based on statistics we all know someone who's chosen to take an *exit* door out of their marriage in hopes of winning something better by playing *let's make a deal*. Most of them will tell you they fell for a lie and ended up swimming in a moat. You and I have the opportunity to head the sewage off at the pass if we rise up as queens of our domain and declare war against the things that threaten our kingdom. We can bring peace back into our palace and take back what's been stolen from us over time. We can turn our future around if we slam all the doors and throw away the keys. Then we can back up, re-evaluate, and start over with the king by our side and a new royal reality.

WILL YOU SAY "NO" TO THE DOOR?

Today, I'm grateful Dan and I made the commitment before we said "I do" to the idea that marriage was a one-way door. Before things ever got tough, we committed to the *no door* policy and it's been the hope we've clung to when our *happily ever after* was in danger. Some of you reading this book didn't start there and most couples don't. I want to encourage you that it's okay. I'm not sure why or how we even knew to take that step, but I'm grateful we can teach other couples from our experience. If you've never made that decree or if you've taken an *exit* door before, it's not too late to bar up the doors and make a new commitment to love for a lifetime. You don't ever have to choose the possibility of getting something better behind a trapdoor over the commitment to a *forever* love story. Unlike the contestants on *Let's Make a Deal*, you don't have to end up with a dud. Let me stop here and say there are times in extenuating circumstances where a *door* must be opened in the case of abuse, but those doors should be the exception to the rule and not the norm. The great news is, it's never too late to redefine what you will and will not do to get where you want to go in your relationship. The choice is yours.

Together, you can remodel and change the floor plans of your castle by building a solid foundation for a palace. The foundation of any building must be poured first before anything else can be built. The *foundation* is the covenant or commitment to the promise of staying in the marriage even when it gets tough no matter what.

THE FOUNDATION = THE COVENANT

You and your spouse poured the foundation of your marriage on your wedding day when you said your vows. Your entire relationship is built on your determination to keep those promises. If your dedication to the covenant of your marriage is strong, the foundation of the palace won't crack when things get hard. If the commitment to the covenant is weak, the foundation will crumble, creating potential for the walls of your marriage to come crashing down.

Compromises must be made, and conversations have to happen to keep the door of divorce closed.

The longer Dan and I are married the more we grow to understand the cost involved in making a marriage work. In the early years, as our narrative began to unfold, we realized we had to make sacrifices or things would unravel. Often marriages begin to fall apart when one partner starts to feel disappointed in the other over unmet expectations. The glue that stops the cracks from forming over unrealistic expectations is the understanding that no one person's existence is for the sole purpose of meeting the needs or expectations of another. To think so is a false belief system. When one or both people in a marriage are disappointed and begin looking at the faults of their mate or their own unmet desires, they lose sight of the bigger picture. The bigger picture is the commitment to the covenant of never opening *the DOOR* and leaving. Compromises must be made, and conversations have to happen to keep the door of divorce closed. Then together you can have the marriage you both desire.

Many couples we've coached have come to us after having spent their entire married lives running from one wall in their castle to the next, trying to hold it all together without ever realizing the fractures were in the foundation. They're the reason the relationship is crumbling. They've reached desperation in trying to find the knob to the door for a way out. Let's consider King Solomon's words. He's often referred to historically as the wisest king that ever lived, and this is what he had to say about making vows and entering into a sacred covenant like marriage. In Proverbs 20:25, he states,

It is a trap for a person to declare quickly, "This is sacred," and only later to have second thoughts about the vows. (ISV)

Fractures in the foundations of broken relationships occur because the things we need to know about building a peaceful palace versus a war-torn castle are rarely taught. For that reason, many marriages are in a constant, captive state of chaos and couples have no idea what to do.

They don't know how to fortify their kingdom and soon realize their marriage is a house of cards. Are you one of those couples? If so, your first goal is to realize marriage doesn't just happen. A glorious palace is planned meticulously and built with care. If you're not married yet, this book is perfect timing for helping you obtain your future peace. If you're already married, it's not too late to consider the cost involved, gather the tools you need, and start remodeling what you've got. Luke 14:28-30 says,

> *For which of you, desiring to build a tower, does not first sit down and count the cost, whether he has enough to complete it? Otherwise, when he has laid a foundation and is not able to finish, all who see it begin to mock him, saying, "This man began to build and was not able to finish." (ESV)*

We have to exercise wisdom and consider the cost when building anything. The floor plans have to be drawn. A firm foundation must be laid. Then the walls of the structure can be built. Finally, the roof or covering must be placed over the entire estate for protection. Even if your marriage has been built for some time or if you're just getting started, we all know from time to time a palace has to be refurbished. With each passing year, we have to adjust to the elements and storms as they come. No matter what, the goal remains the same... marriage and love for a lifetime. If you're like most women, we all love to paint and remodel, so let's get started and dig a little deeper into the foundation of the covenant of marriage.

WHAT IS A COVENANT?

According to author J. Maurice Wright, covenants are "a written document or verbal statement that binds individuals to an agreement, with blessings given for keeping it and curses inflicted for breaking it." From the beginning of time covenants have been used to mark oaths meant to be fool proof. They symbolize an unshakable, trustworthy promise.

A COVENANT = A CONCRETE PROMISE

If the promise is broken, then the persons involved will experience the consequences that will cause curses to fall into their lives as a result. From all the couples we know who have chosen to walk through the door of divorce, every area of their life was affected by overwhelming chaos. We can see it in the moats surrounding us full of broken homes and children from the revolving door of divorce. The commitment to a marriage is meant to be the concrete promise we pour into the foundation of our palace. Staying committed to that promise makes the marriage rock solid.

WHAT ARE THE INGREDIENTS IN THE CONCRETE?

The ingredients in the concrete of your foundation are the wedding day promises, "for better or for worse, for richer or for poorer, in sickness and in health, till death do you part." Even if you stated different vows, vows are the foundation of *forever*. As shared, Dan and I started our foundation with the promise we made not to consider the *D-word*, and you can too. The concrete you and I pour into that foundation is based on the principles that marriage is a business, a friendship between equal partners, and a lifelong sacrificial commitment to the success of the relationship. It's a business because it involves the combining and accounting of possessions and a financial plan to remain in the black and not the red. It's a friendship where two people become one in every area of lives. It's a sacrifice, because any relationship that stands the test of time is based on love with a commitment to compromise and a dedication to work things out no matter what. In our *marital and premarital* coaching, we dig even deeper into historical covenants where couples discover how those three principles work in a marriage in real life situations and what they symbolize in the wedding ceremony. For more details, go to www.ChaosOrPeace.us.

Like beautiful pictures in a gallery, our marriage can become an artistic masterpiece.

Once the foundation is poured, the most beautiful parts of the palace can be built. That's where we'll spend most of our time for the remainder of this book. Together, we'll gather the information we need to complete the floor plans we want. We'll examine a series of questions that every queen should be willing to answer to build her palace. By applying these concepts, you and your knight in shining armor can move into a beautiful palace. When you and I have beautiful marriages, it allows us to help other couples change their chaos into peace through our example. Like beautiful pictures in a gallery, our marriage can become an artistic masterpiece other people will stand and gaze upon with admiration!

CROWNING POINTS

- ♛ Eliminate the D-word from your vocabulary
- ♛ Let go of unmet expectations
- ♛ Never fall for the trapdoor or greener grass
- ♛ Marriage is a business, a friendship, and a sacrifice
- ♛ Stand firm on the foundation of the covenant

Now we're going to climb from the foundation of your palace to the rooftop. If you've ever seen or visited a grand palace in person, the most amazing part of this architectural beauty is the pointed towers and spires and the decorative cap stones that have been placed at the top that cover and protect the entire palace. It's like the icing on a wedding cake! Just as the foundation is crucial at the bottom, the roof is necessary at the top. Without it, when the storms of life come, it leaks, and the walls fall down.

To help you in this journey, we offer a free assessment at our website www.ChaosOrPeace.us. Follow me to Chapter 2 as I share about a fierce battle Dan and I faced together that started in our fifth year of marriage. The pain and glory changed our love story but solidified the covering over our lives and made us who we are today. It writes like a soap opera but ends with a *Happily Ever After...*

Chapter 2

ARE YOU MEANT FOR ROYALTY?

Royalty and fame are intriguing to every human being. We all desire to reach some level of greatness. Hollywood has played a role in drawing us in to the stories they tell leaving us with a yearning for notoriety on the world's stage. Many people either long for fame and fortune with their name in lights or grit and glory with their name in the history books. We all aspire to leave a legacy to be remembered. That desire drives the decisions we make every day from people like you and me all the way up the ladder to powerful world leaders. In this chapter, I want to share my personal journey with you. It gave me the name I'd always wanted and changed my life and our marriage forever. It taught me who I really am and confirmed my right to claim my throne as queen of my home alongside the king that I married. When we discovered the truth about our identity, it placed the crowning roof over our palace. I think you'll be surprised by the fairy tale ending because our story could change your story!

WHERE DID I GET MY ROOTS?

My life began on a humble little farm with cows, horses, chickens, dogs and cats, and a raccoon for a pet. I know that doesn't sound like the *royal family*, but trust me, I thought it was. Even though we lived in the country and didn't really have a lot of wealth, we gave the impression we did, and image in a small town is everything. I remember being one of the first families to have a microwave oven. Hot food coming out in seconds was the most amazing thing I'd ever seen, and I'll never forget the day my chore of washing dishes was abolished. My dad came home with a new electric dishwasher and I had been liberated!

We soon became the envy of the entire community after dad built us an in-ground swimming pool from the dirt up! Everybody wanted to be my friend, especially in the summer. In my mind, people were beginning to think I was *somebody* important. Truthfully, I was just a country girl with big ideas, but I fell for the lie of making popularity my priority. I learned wherever I went in a twenty-mile radius all I had to do was drop my dad's name. People immediately knew who I was or at least recognized my dad as the wheeling dealing cowboy entrepreneur that he was. He had his hands in every business deal he could work. I took pride in his name because it earned me the identity of being known as *my father's* daughter and it opened doors.

After graduating from high school and then college, I found myself accepting a job in Atlanta, Georgia. I left everything I'd ever known and all my country roots, except for the ones that were bleached blonde, and headed to the biggest city in the south. It was a time in my life when all my friends were getting married and settling down, and I too longed to be the bride and not the bride's maid.

In this new metropolis where I was a complete stranger, what was a girl to do? I started looking in all the wrong places the city had to offer for a husband. I soon found the search to be empty and pointless. There were plenty of available guys, but none of them were the noble type I'd dreamed of. Then I started dating a guy from my hometown. I'd actually grown up dreaming of becoming his wife from the time I was five years old when we won a Little Mr. and Ms. Beauty pageant together. He was my escort. Dating him seemed like a fairy tale come true. He was from a well-to-do family in town, and we'd spent our entire school career hanging out in the same friend group. He would often say to me, "We could get married since we both want the same things; a nice house, two nice cars, and a couple of kids." The problem was he and I didn't really want the same future. I'd grown up in a house with two cars and two kids, and it didn't really bring us happiness. Despite this revelation, we continued to date. Since it was a long-distance relationship, and we weren't married yet, I decided to try something new and head to the local church. After all, I'd grown up in church.

WHERE CAN A GIRL FIND LOVE?

I was determined to visit a mega church with a reputation for being a matchmaking oasis. On the day I set out to attend, I got lost and ended up somewhere else by mistake. My country roots gave me no sense of direction on the city streets. I was completely turned around. As I sat at a traffic light in front of a large church on the corner, I heard a voice inside my head say, "Why don't you just go to that church?" Since this was not my original plan, I argued with the voice and kept driving. As I glanced at the clock, I soon realized I was running out of time. I decided to turn around and go back to the corner church after all. Fortunately, my steps were being ordered that day. Surprisingly, the people were friendly and welcomed me with open arms, so I decided to stay.

Just a few weeks later, on a Sunday morning, a handsome guy saw me from across the room. I never saw him, but he determined at first glance he would ask me out on a date. He leaned over to a friend and asked who I was. His friend gave him my name but explained I was dating someone from my hometown. This guy was undeterred. He looked at his friend and quoted his favorite Bible verse, "I can do all things through Christ who gives me strength." He began to pray for me in the weeks that followed.

Three months later, on a Saturday morning, it suddenly hit me I was wasting time in a relationship that was never meant to be a part of my future. I called the hometown guy and ended it. The next day as I stepped into a classroom at the church, my eyes met the eyes of a handsome guy and my heart skipped a beat. I remember thinking to myself, "He's going to be important in your life". I had no idea just how important. That night the verse he'd quoted a few months back came to pass. He asked me out on our first date. In just eleven months we were engaged. Three months later, Dan and I said, "I do"! Everyone in my hometown thought I was marrying up. They all drove for hours to see a country girl marry a prince from the big city. We said our vows, I tossed the bouquet, and we were off to our fairy tale life!

IF I'M NOT MY FATHER'S DAUGHTER, WHO AM I?

The palace roof, in all its glory, is the overall arching factor in an estate's ability to stand the test of time.

I imagined after the bouquet was thrown and the guests were gone, I would have my *happily ever after* story. However, I soon realized I wasn't *royalty* after all. I couldn't use the line about being my father's daughter anymore. No one in Atlanta had ever heard of my dad. Even though I was from the state just next door, I was a foreigner of sorts to the people in my new town. In my mind southerners were all the same because we're all from below the Mason Dixon line. I soon learned differently on my first day of teaching school as one of my new students raised his hand to ask a question. To my surprise, he said, "I just need to ask you one thing. Where are you from, Texas?" I was not in Alabama anymore. In fact, I had no idea where I was or who I was. I was no longer *my father's daughter* but *my husband's wife*. I knew how to cook and clean because those were things I'd grown up doing, but I had no idea how to be a wife or meet anyone's expectations, not even my own. This drove me to search for answers about identity and my role as a woman in marriage.

WHAT DOES A ROOF HAVE TO DO WITH MARRIAGE?

Just as the foundation is fundamental to a palace, the roof is crucial to covering and protecting it all. The palace roof, in all its glory, is the overall arching factor in an estate's ability to stand the test of time. It's the defining, finishing element to whom you and your husband will be in your life together. It defines your identity.

THE COVERING = YOUR IDENTITY

As I found myself in the middle of an identity crisis, there was no job description, and I had no job experience. Since I could no longer use the line of being my father's daughter, I had to learn how to become my husband's wife. With no script on how to play my starring role as a palace queen, I felt lost. All I had was a heart full of love and a mind full of romantic ideas. I was faced with the dilemma of figuring it all out alone. Little did I know, in my complete frustration, I was about to collide head on with the power of *identity*, and it would completely change not only my life but Dan's life forever. Dan and I soon found ourselves in the middle of a tragedy where information came at warp speed. Crisis has a way of doing that. It creates an opportunity for rapid, life-changing growth. The minefield we found ourselves in, forced us to quickly learn who we really were as husband and wife. It gave us a new identity and established the roof over our palace.

What is a roof made of?

Our fairy tale turned into a tragedy when my father died suddenly without a *Last Will and Testament*, creating an abundance of complicated circumstances. By law, his estate went into probate under the protection of the state. A *probate* is "a set period of time when the deceased debts are paid, the heirs determined, and the remainder of his possessions divided equally among them." Since my parents had divorced just two years earlier, my sister and I were the only heirs. We all assumed it would be a standard six-month process. However, as time began to slip away and spin out of control, two years into sorting through all the chaos it took a turn for the worse. Someone declared they had witnessed a Will written by my father. They claimed I wasn't in the Will because I was not my father's daughter. Even though there had never been a Will, the statement created a legal firestorm. My sister decided to sue for my inheritance.

I was in shock. After thirty years, it was the first time I'd ever heard this story and not something I could ever have imagined happening. After all, I had always found pride in being called my father's daughter. Since there was no legal precedence for this kind of case, the magistrate pondered whether to force me to take a DNA test to determine who I really was. The courts couldn't decide if it even mattered since my dad had raised me as his own and believed I was his daughter until the day he died. I was shaken by the events that were unfolding. Soon, I found myself so devastated that one day I filled the tub, put our son in his room with a gate, and climbed into the water with the determination to take my own life. I was in my second trimester of pregnancy with our daughter at the time, but all I could think about was stopping the unbearable pain. I believed if I would just sink into the warm water and inhale, with one deep breath it would all be over, and the pain would stop.

I didn't know who I was anymore, and there was nowhere to hide. As I slowly began to lower myself down into the water just inches away from inhaling, I heard a voice inside my head say, "Get up and get help now before you destroy your life and the lives of everyone you love." I snapped back into reality. It was the same voice I'd heard the day I went looking for the *matchmaking* church and ended up at the church where I met my husband. It didn't steer me in the wrong direction then, and on this day that same voice was saving my life and the life of my unborn daughter. I suddenly realized what I was doing. I got up and called for help and headed into intense counseling. I really did want to survive, and my motivation was my daughter's future. She was a gift and I wanted her to live. Dan and I also started marriage counseling to keep us from walking out *the DOOR*. We needed help to survive this horrible storm. It was a process of putting our lives back together one piece at a time even though the legal matters were still unresolved. Our commitment to the promises we had made on our wedding day is what held us together as our love grew numb.

Over the next five years, we not only faced the legal battles but many personal crises as well. We had confronted death, a family breakup, an identity crisis, and my attempted suicide. The next tragedy was our daughter's sudden illness from a mis-filled prescription that triggered an incurable blood disease. A year and a half later, she was healed. Two years later she had a freak accident. It crushed her right index finger requiring two reconstructive surgeries. There were medical bills and mounting legal expenses, and our marriage was on life support. The only place we found peace was in prayer and the miraculous things that no one could explain that only God could have done. We would never have survived, and our marriage would have fallen apart without God hovering over us as the roof over our war-torn castle. He protected us when nothing else could.

CAN WE EXCHANGE ONE IDENTITY FOR ANOTHER?

At the six-and-a-half-year mark of the probate of my father's estate, I heard that voice again. By this time, I knew it was God. He made it clear I was to volunteer to take a DNA test so my identity could be determined once and for all. I had no idea who I was, but the DNA test would finally answer the question. The papers were signed, and the date was set. What happened on test day is nothing short of supernatural! It might even challenge you to consider the actual existence of God if you don't already believe.

On the day of the test near the seven-year mark, Dan and I sat at the medical center waiting for it to open. I was struggling with fear and heartbreak as I began to fall apart. My mind flashed back over our long and treacherous journey. I realized for the first time it had been a lot like a slow and painful death to everything I had ever known as *normal.* We had to learn to die to ourselves repeatedly as we were forced into life changing circumstances with nowhere to turn but God. The journey had been filled with us learning what it meant to let go of things we had trusted in. My identity as my father's daughter had been pillaged and taken. On this day, it was as if the curtain was being pulled back, so I could really understand what God had been doing over the last seven years. I also began to realize what he had done two thousand years ago when he sacrificed his son's life on a cross.

Jesus had left what he knew in Heaven to come to the earth as the son of Mary and Joseph, the earthly parents who raised him. At age thirty he gave up his position as their son and started his ministry where he proclaimed his true identity as the Son of God. I, too, had lost my identity as my father's daughter at age thirty. As a result of his public proclamation, Jesus was unjustly accused and dragged from court to court as the rulers tried to determine who he really was. I, too, was falsely accused of destroying my father's Will. I'd been dragged from court to court as the judges tried to decide who I really was. Jesus was beaten repeatedly and ridiculed by the people he had loved. I, too, had been beaten down and ridiculed by people I trusted and loved. Jesus' own brothers and sisters wanted nothing to do with him when he started his ministry. My only sister had turned her back on me claiming I did not deserve to be her sister or share in my inheritance. People Jesus trusted betrayed him, until they saw him crucified and his identity was miraculously exposed. On this day, after all the betrayal, I was dying to whom I'd been. I would finally know who I really was.

What happened on DNA day?

Everything changed for me that day. As we left home that morning headed to the lab, I grabbed a book from the shelf I'd been reading. It was called *The Gift for All People* by Max Lucado. While Dan and I sat waiting my turn, I began to struggle with fear of facing what lay ahead. I suddenly remembered the book and pulled it from my bag. As I opened it to the page holding a bookmark, at the top it read, "God's Bounteous Grace." I stopped and reflected on the grace that had gotten us to this point. Then as my eyes moved down the page, I was awe struck when I suddenly realized what was written. It was as if God had just sent me a personal text message. It read...

> *For you no longer have to worry about who your Farther is; for you are an heir to MY throne through my son. Galatians 4:7 (Max Lucado, The Gift)*

In a single moment it was as if every cloud was gone, the rain had stopped, the sun was shining, and the birds were singing. My life was instantaneously and miraculously transformed. It was no coincidence the book was titled *The Gift* because I had just received the greatest gift my Father in Heaven had to offer me! For the first time in my life I realized all those years I'd found such pride in being called *my father's* daughter, I was actually the daughter of a great and mighty King! I was an heir to an inheritance far bigger than my earthly dad had possessed. God was handing me a legacy that could not be taken away in a court of law or contained on a piece of paper.

> *Let us thank the God and Father of our Lord Jesus Christ. (Because) It was through His loving kindness that we were born again to a new life and have a hope that never dies. This hope is ours because Jesus was raised from the dead. We will receive the great things (inheritance) that we have been promised. They are being kept safe in Heaven for us. They are pure and will not pass away. They will never be lost... 1 Peter 1:3-5 (NLV)*

I knew from attending church the story of how God had sent his son to the earth as a sacrifice, so we could have a faith-based relationship with him. Over the last six and a half years, I'd seen too many miracles not to know that he was real. Our salvation is only gained through faith in who Jesus said he was and the power of his death, burial, and resurrection. Historically, in the places he went people called him a miracle worker. Dan and I had come to realize that he really was miraculous. Nothing else could explain the things he had done in the tragedy we had faced or how we had survived it all without his presence.

At that moment, God had adopted me as his daughter, and all my earthly identities had been wiped away. I became his daughter when He took me as his own and connected me to his royal bloodline. He was my real Father. I had been grafted into a new vine of a different family tree. I was royalty in His eyes, and nothing would ever change that or take that away from me. I was His and He was mine!

Adoption seals our identity making us noble, royal, heirs.

God had been the voice in my head directing my steps to Dan the day I got lost and ended up at a different church than originally planned. He was the voice who had saved my life the day the enemy wanted to drown me in a tub. He was the one who had healed our daughter twice. He'd been by our side through the entire journey to my noble identity. His love and sacrifice had created the opportunity for our adoption into the royal family of the King. Adoption seals our identity making us noble, royal, heirs worthy to reign our kingdom.

> *God sent him to buy freedom for us who were slaves to the law, so that he could adopt us as his very own children. Galatians 4:5 (NLT)*

The results of the DNA test no longer mattered to me because my identity had been divinely determined and the roof above our palace was complete.

CROWNING POINTS

- ♛ Every man and woman was created for royalty
- ♛ Adoption through faith seals your DNA
- ♛ Choose to believe and God becomes the roof of the palace
- ♛ He protects us in the storms of life when nothing else will

The probate ended, and the estate was soon dissolved. The total time had been seven years. The number *seven* in the Bible means "spiritual perfection." God's work was complete in giving me my new royal identity as a daughter of the King. I hope you'll follow me to the next chapter where we'll dig deeper into the symbolism of royal adoption and discover the rest of the story. I think you'll be amazed!

Chapter 3

WILL YOU CHOOSE TO BE ADOPTED?

What's in a name? Throughout biblical history, God named things, changed the names of places and people, and referred to himself by specific names at least nine-hundred and forty-four times. The names he gave people identified character, or a life's purpose, or a circumstance under which the person had been born. On some occasions God renamed people to represent a new covenant with them to seal their new identity. As our seven-year ordeal with my father's estate ended, I began to see how God had been changing my character to match my name throughout every part of the journey. Even though my mom had named me with no spiritual intent, she had given me the name Lydia Faith at birth. A woman in the New Testament from Thyatira named Lydia became the first European to embrace faith in Christ. She was a woman who sold *purple*. Purple fabric was considered one of the most expensive linens a person could own, usually only affordable to the royals. The name *Lydia* in Hebrew means "of the noble kind". I had no idea what my name meant until we had branded our ministry's print media *Living in Nobility*. The name *Faith* means "a belief or trust in something for which there is no proof, miraculous without question." God knew from the day I was conceived I would one day face an identity crisis, and he would have to perform the miraculous for me to survive. Psalm 68:5 states,

He is a father to the fatherless and an advocate for widows. God rules from his holy palace.

My Father knew in the midst of devastation I'd find myself father-less. From his palace he ruled that when that happened, I would clearly know who I was created to be. I am a seller of purple like Lydia in the Scriptures. Through my story of faith, I want to help women become the royal queen they were created to be. Why? Because the only place to find peace, is in your true identity as a daughter of the King.

WHY IS THERE NO PEACE?

We can all admit that there is both the presence of good and evil in the world. It's been here since the beginning of time. You can see it in every movie and fairy tale. In *Snow White*, it's the wicked queen. In *Cinderella*, it's the stepmother and stepsisters. In *Sleeping Beauty* it's the wicked old witch. In *The Avengers*, it's the Masters of Evil. In the Garden of Eden where the first wedding took place, it was Satan, the master of all evil. He came to destroy the first marriage and believe it or not he is also coming after yours.

WHY DOES THE ENEMY WANT TO DESTROY MY MARRIAGE?

It all started in the Garden of Eden where the first married couple were wed. Their names were Adam and Eve, and we'll examine how their life together unfolded throughout this book. Since they were the first couple to marry, we can learn a lot from their story. Everything was perfect until their arch enemy led them down the wrong path, into the wrong decisions, and out the garden gate for good. He hated the royal birthright given to them by the King of Kings. Out of God's love for them, he gave Adam and Eve complete dominion over everything on the earth as a part of their heritage. Satan wanted that power. He knew it was something he could never have because he had committed treason against God. The Scripture says God came down and walked with the newlyweds in the garden daily. When Satan saw Adam and Eve living in close companionship with God the Father, he determined to rob them of their happy, harmonious home. His actions were no different from the days of old when some other villain or vigilante decided to overthrow the royal throne and steal the kingdom.

Satan knew if he could cause Adam and Eve to doubt their Father, he could take their royal position as rulers. He purposed to lead them into an identity crisis, so they would search for their identity in other things. If they followed him, he could overthrow their position as children of the King. They'd hand over their power to rule the earth, and he'd take the dominion God meant to be theirs. This is the same trick Satan's using today. Everywhere we look people are searching for their identity in anything they can find versus living as the royalty they were really created to be. This is the *trap door* Satan offers every married couple. He offered us door #1, door #2, and door #3 during our seven-year trek, and we had to fight the temptation to trade in what we had for something different. There were seasons I thought it couldn't get any worse. In my pain, I thought God was nowhere to be found. It suddenly became crystal clear the day I opened *The Gift* that he'd been there all along because he loved me as a Father loves a daughter.

God had been revealing the very nature of his presence within each challenge we'd faced. Unfortunately, during our struggles his full identity had gone unrecognized until that defining DNA moment. Instantaneously I understood who He really was and had been since the beginning of time. In the days of castles and palaces a banner hung over the great estate, marking the identity of the king and queen with the family crest. In our journey, God's many names had been marking our path to that fateful day when my identity as a daughter would be affirmed. God had literally placed a banner over my life, revealing his full nature in those final moments. He was *Jehovah Nissi* which means "the Lord my banner." I was a daughter of a King, and his banner hung over our household just as the banners hung over the kingdoms of old. In Song of Songs 2:4 declares,

His banner over me was love. (ESV)

God had been walking this journey with us, patiently covering us with his love every step of the way. Amid our financial challenges he was *Jehovah Jireh*, "the Lord will provide." He made provision for us to pay for all the legal and medical expenses we'd faced without us accumulating debt. In all the chaos in our castle, he had been *Jehovah Shalom*, "the Lord is Peace." In every challenge, every loss, every illness or injury, his supernatural peace had sustained us. Without it, we never would have survived. Philippians 4:7 states,

Then God's peace, which goes beyond anything we can imagine, will guard your thoughts and emotions through Christ Jesus. (GWT)

As the battles raged, He had watched over it all as *El Shaddai*, "the Lord God Almighty." Even when we felt hopeless, he had been standing with all his power overseeing the war. When it appeared all would be lost, even on the day I determined to take my own life, he had come running to my rescue. In his love, he had gathered me up out of that watery grave. In Hebrew, he's known as *Jehovah Rapha*, "the Lord who heals us." He had healed my broken heart. He had restored our daughter from an incurable disease and healed her finger with a simple touch of his hand. On the day of the DNA test, he called me by name and marked me as his own. He was saying I am your *Abba*, "Father". He was undeniably confirming I was and had always been my Father's daughter. Instantaneously, I gained my noble identity in him.

He was our *Yehoshua* in Hebrew, "the Lord is our salvation." He had saved us in our desperate cries for help. As we realized who he really was, we realized who we really are. The exciting news is he sees every person as his child, and he wants to adopt not just me, but you too. If you and I choose to be adopted and enter into a relationship with him, he sees us as his very own children. We are his, and he loves us as his own flesh and blood. Romans 8:17 declares,

Now if we are children, then we are heirs—heirs of God and co-heirs with Christ (our brother), if indeed we share in his (Christ's) sufferings in order that we may also share in his glory.

Our Abba Father lovingly gives us a new identity when we raise him up as the roof over our palace and the covering over our lives. He is the glorious spire on top of it all when we allow him to rule over our kingdom. When we choose to let him become our Father, he becomes the roof over our lives! He is *El Elyon*, "the Lord Most High!"

WHAT IS ADOPTION?

Adoption means "to choose or take as one's own; to take and rear the child of other parents as one's own child, specifically by formal adoption." All over the world there are orphans longing for parents, hoping to be adopted by someone they can trust that will love them forever.

> When we choose to let God become our Father, he becomes the roof that covers us from the chaos that surrounds us!

Adoption has no limits. It shows no favor. Families who've lovingly adopted never notice the difference between their adopted children and their biological sons and daughters.

One of my favorite adoption stories comes from our own family. Our nephew and his beautiful wife have seven children. They had a son early in the first couple of years of marriage. Then they began to feel the tug towards adoption and decided to take the leap of faith. They chose to adopt outside their race because the need is so great, and God had captured their hearts with a desire for domestic adoption. Regardless of the difference in their skin color, as their first adopted daughter came home, it was quickly evident their love was no different between her and the son they had birthed. Next, they gave birth to another daughter. As time passed, it was as if their lives were being perfectly woven together like a tapestry creating an amazing work of art. Again, they began to feel the tug of adoption a second time. This time, they were offered the opportunity to adopt twin girls. Twins seemed a little overwhelming, but in a short time, God changed their hearts. Their twins were scheduled to arrive as a wonderful Christmas blessing! Sadly, on the last day the law allows the mother chose to terminate her adoption plans. It was a devastating blow. My nephew and his family wept as if they had experienced the death of a child they had birthed.

Their loss profoundly offers a small glimpse of how our Father in Heaven loves us in our orphan state and wants to bring us home. When we're lost, he weeps. He desires to adopt us into his family. Miraculously, after their loss, God brought four more beautiful children into their lives. Today he and his wife and their seven adorable children love and live as one big happy family, seeing no difference between the children they birthed and the ones they've adopted. Their adoption story offers us a picture of how a new vine grafted into the trunk of another tree, in a short time becomes one sturdy, unshakable family tree. The lines where they were grafted together have completely disappeared. As a trans-racial family, their home exudes the beauty of adoption and the depth of the spiritual exchange that takes place when we choose to be adopted by our Heavenly Father. When we join his royal family in faith, he loves us completely and sees us no differently than he sees Jesus, his son.

When Jesus came to the earth, lived, died, and rose from the grave, his resurrection built the bridge for our adoption to a Father who can be trusted and will never leave us or abandon us without an inheritance. Historical references show Jesus lived without ever committing any wrongdoing. Remaining sinless made him the perfect payment for our adoption. In reality, adoption can cost tens of thousands of dollars. This is why many families never choose to adopt. God paid in full the cost of our adoption with the life of his son.

Historically, every year during the Jewish holiday of Passover, the father of each family would bring a perfect, unblemished lamb to sacrifice at the temple. This was done to abolish the family's sins that were committed over the last year. That unblemished sacrifice represented the most expensive thing they had to offer for the payment of their sins. It meant their sins were completely forgiven. Unfortunately, it didn't help them get free from the temptation to sin, so the ritual had to be repeated every year. As a result, God allowed difficult circumstances throughout the Old Testament to magnify their overwhelming need for a Savior who could finally free them from their propensity toward wrong choices. In the New Testament, He provided the final solution to their problem. He sent Jesus by earthly birth to become the unblemished sacrificial lamb for all sins committed by all people in the past, present, and future. God sacrificed the most priceless thing he had to offer as payment for our spiritual adoption.

WILL YOU CHOOSE BELIEF OR UNBELIEF?

Jesus represented the unblemished animal that had to be sacrificed for sin as he hung on a cross with his arms outstretched. Historical references say there were two thieves crucified with Jesus that day. Each hung on a cross on either side of him as he hung in the middle. It's recorded that one thief chose to believe Jesus was the son of God. He entered into a relationship with Him through faith as he took his final breaths. The other mocked Jesus and chose not to believe, and he died unforgiven in his guilt and shame. In reality, Jesus hung in the middle of belief and unbelief. He was the bridge between the two choices, and through him God was asking us to become blood brothers and sisters with Christ. The shedding of his blood symbolized God offering to make a blood covenant with us so our old identity could be washed away. As stated in Chapter 1, a covenant is an unbreakable, unshakable promise. His sacrifice gives us the opportunity to take on a new name as a daughter to our Abba Father.

WHY WOULD GOD SEND HIS SON TO DIE FOR YOU?

God loved you enough to make the biggest sacrifice he had to offer, so he could have a personal relationship with you. Though our marriage covenant requires trust that our spouse will keep their commitment, our Father has proven his dedication to us with his son's life making it unbreakable. By giving his only son to become the sacrificial lamb, he offers us a covenant that can never be broken. If you believe, you can enter a relationship with God based on faith and trust. At that moment, you become royalty by adoption. All you have to do is believe.

The day my identity was determined, my royal heritage was sealed. Your Father wants to do the same for you. When we willingly place ourselves in a covenant of faith with him, it means we're placing ourselves underneath his covering, and he becomes the permanent roof over our palace. He covers us with his protection, his power, and his royal name just as the noble king of any kingdom did for his children years ago. We can change our chaotic castle into a peaceful palace no matter what circumstances we face if we allow him to become the roof that protects us from the chaos that surrounds us. Romans 8:15 proclaims,

The Spirit you received does not make you slaves, so that you live in fear again; rather, the spirit you received brought about your adoption to sonship. And by him we cry, "Abba, Father".

According to the Scripture, everything changes when we're adopted. Your adoption makes you and your spouse rulers over your home, giving you a kingdom where you can flourish. As you move into the *palace* life God has designed for you, you begin to look at the world completely different. That new perspective helps us understand who we really are in every area of our lives. It's all about the *bigger picture*. The bigger picture is grounded in the marriage covenants you've made to one another. If you've already crossed that bridge of faith into a relationship with Christ, you're already adopted. If not, understanding your bloodline is crucial to your *happily ever after* future.

WILL YOU STEP INTO ROYALTY?

Our greatest desire in this book is to help you find your authentic identity not just as a wife but as a daughter. Why? Let's face it, life is hard. Mating and relating in marriage are hard, and some days it seems impossible. Without the covering of God over our life as the roof over our palace, the probability of the walls crashing down when the battles start to rage is extremely high. Every couple has a divine purpose. We were created to live in nobility and rule our kingdom well. As Jesus taught in Matthew 6:33, he challenges us to do just that. It states,

> But seek ye first the kingdom of God, and his righteousness; and all these things shall be added unto you.

Many interpret this verse to mean we are to seek the things of God, and he will give us what we need. This is not what God was saying at all. Instead, we have to look at the original Greek to learn the real meaning of what God meant. To *seek* actually means "to demand or take by force". The word *kingdom* "is not to be confused with a Heavenly kingdom but an earthly kingdom that you've been given charge over." In other words, as sons and daughters of the King, we are to seek or take by force the dominion our enemy Satan has stolen from us. We were created to rule the domain or household our Father has given us by living in the nobility found in our identity as his child.

Stepping into your purpose is as simple as admitting you need God's help. You can choose to believe God sent his son Jesus to give you victory. His victory over death and the grave makes you victorious over your challenges giving you a future in him. All you have to do is walk across the bridge he built by believing and putting your faith in Jesus. You then become your Heavenly Father's child.

Are you prepared to turn your castle into a palace and stabilize the future of your marriage? Simply read and follow the steps below and pray the prayer to receive your new identity in Christ. Your adoption will change the course of your life and marriage forever!

THE GUIDELINES FOR ROYAL ADOPTION

C onfess that you make mistakes and cannot do life or marriage without God's help.

O pen your mind to the idea God created you, He loves you, and He wants to be your Abba Father.

V eto any thoughts that you can do this alone or you don't need help to make your life, marriage, and even your parenting work.

E nter into a relationship with your Father, by simply choosing to believe and trust Him.

N ever doubt that it's this simple. He reached down to you by sending His Son to die so that you can be adopted and move into His camp.

A llow Him to love you just the way you are, no matter what you've done or where you've been. His love is free to you if you choose to receive it.

N ever fear the loss of your identity or inheritance. When you become part of His family, you seal your birthright and heritage forever.

T ake Him by the hand and walk into your new identity as His daughter! You can choose to step into royalty.

You can pray this prayer of faith and believe in your new identity.

Dear Abba Father, I cannot save myself or my marriage without you. I know you sent your son to die for my mistakes in order to provide a way for my adoption into your family. I want to walk across the bridge of faith that Jesus created through his death, burial, and resurrection. I'm asking you to adopt me and make me your child. Please forgive me for all the wrong choices I've made. Please become the banner over my life and my palace. Please become my Lord and my Savior. I believe in your kingdom. Thank you for calling me your own and making me an heir to the inheritance you have for me. Thank you for adopting me and giving me a new identity in you. Amen

(If you prayed this prayer of commitment please fill out the form on the following page as a confirmation of your adoption.)

CROWNING POINTS

- ♛ Names are important to God
- ♛ God's many names prove his character and establish our trust
- ♛ Adoption solidifies our identity in Him
- ♛ Identity gives us the right to rule our kingdom in nobility
- ♛ Being adopted changes everything

Your Adoption Papers

_____

Name: _____

DOB: _____

Date of Adoption: _____

Parent adopting this child:

Abba   Father

Jehovah Nissi   The Lord Your Banner

Jehovah Shalom   The Lord Is Peace

El Shaddai   The Lord God Almighty

El Elyon   The Lord Most High

Jehovah Rapha   The Lord Who Heals Us

Jehovah Jireh   The Lord Will Provide

Yehoshua   The Lord is our Salvation, Rescuer, and Deliverer

Sealed on this_____day of_____in the year of_____

Chapter 4

WHO AM I IN THE KINGDOM?

After my identity was settled, I was ready to move forward in discovering the details that define my position as the queen of my home. Around that same time, Dan and I were miraculously offered the opportunity of a lifetime. We received an unexpected call from the director of marriage ministries at *Lifeway Christian Resources*. He wanted us to serve as team members at their *Fall Festival of Marriage* conferences the following year. We had started a non-profit ministry during the probate of my father's estate, and we had just released our first album. The Lifeway director had seen it on the desk of a mutual friend and listened to it. There were two songs on the album about marriage. One was the song Dan wrote and proposed with that we later sung in our wedding. The other song was about a broken marriage that I wrote when my parents divorced. Those two songs led to our invitation to join the marriage conference team. We had been ministering to friends whose marriages were in trouble for several years, but until we were given this opportunity, we'd never considered marriage ministry as an official calling on our lives.

We took the job because we cared deeply about the success of other marriages. In the process of preparing, I started getting new clarity from Scripture on marriage. It wasn't that the topics were new, it was the fact that many ideas on marriage are usually taught at face value, and I was digging into the Greek and Hebrew roots and their original meanings. What I discovered blew the castle right out of the water. At the first conference Dan and I realized many couples of all ages and walks of life were searching for answers to questions we had at the beginning of our marriage. They wanted to know how to understand their roles and how to walk in their identity as husband and wife. Even couples married for many years were still living with chaos in their castles finding no answers to the questions they had in order to have peace in their homes.

WHY DID WE DECIDE TO WRITE BOOKS ON MARRIAGE?

The morning after finishing our first Lifeway retreat, I woke to the birds singing at sunrise, and reflected on how God had so graciously walked with us through the entire seven-year probate process. Then it hit me. Our experience was meant to be used for a greater purpose. We believed discovering our true identity could give other couples hope and direction in their search for finding their own. As we stepped into marriage ministry, it was as if we had stepped into the right place, at the right time, doing the miraculous thing we had been created to do. God was calling us to use our past to impact your future!

A couple of weeks later, while spending a lengthy time in prayer, I began to hear questions in my mind I knew couples were asking about their relationships. As they began to unfold, I grabbed a pen and paper to write them down. Funny thing was, the questions came in the form of kings, queens, chaos, and peace, and the title of this book was birthed! I had been a writer my entire life, but God was calling Dan and I to write a book for men and women on marriage. *Marriage Warrior* is our companion book for men and is available on various book sites.

WHAT DOES IT MEAN TO LIVE IN NOBILITY?

I can't wait to share the questions God asked that day and the answers we've found by searching! However, before we march forward, we first need to understand some keywords and their meanings as they relate to our identity from our Father's perspective. Let's first consider the definitions of the newfound titles we receive when we choose to be adopted. The first word is *nobility*. It means, "belonging to a hereditary class by birth or adoption and being of exalted moral character." We've already established that we become nobility when we choose to be adopted by our Abba Father. He takes us just as we are, in our dirty orphan state. As his children we begin to take on his identity and moral character as he loves us and cleans us up.

The word *queen* is defined as "a woman considered the best or most important of her kind; the wife of a king, one who inherits her position by right of marriage or birth". I Peter 1:3-4 confirms this,

Praise be to the God and Father of our Lord Jesus Christ! In his great mercy he has given us new birth into a living hope through the resurrection of Jesus Christ from the dead and into an inheritance that can never perish, spoil, or fade.

In the historical time known as the Renaissance period, medieval kings and queens were the rulers of the day. A good queen, deserving of her crown, carried an inner strength giving her the ability to make good decisions when the king was away. She might be described as a woman who could speak eloquently at appropriate times with wisdom to hold her tongue when required. In her silence she still showed the presence of a forceful self-assurance. A noble queen was a woman of great poise regardless of her outward circumstances. She emanated a radiant light, beauty, and fortitude even in a season of war. Despite what our culture has tried to tell us about the traditional ideas of a wife being outdated and archaic, I found this description to be appealing and applicable to any powerful woman in today's world. I knew this was the kind of wife I wanted to be.

The term *king* is defined "as the male ruler of a country who has inherited the throne from his parents; a person considered to be the best or most important of its kind and the ruler of a kingdom." In medieval times, a good king might be described as one of noble character who was true to his duty. He showed integrity in his leadership, possessing the character of a great and mighty warrior while carrying out his authority over the kingdom. A good king makes decisions based on what's best for everyone else under his palace roof. He willingly lays down his life to protect his domain if necessary. According to that definition, I can imagine we'd all love for our husbands to lead like noble kings, willing to do whatever it takes to protect and defend like a mighty warrior. Again, Scripture supports this idea in Ephesians 5:25,

Husbands love your wives, just as Christ also loved the church and gave Himself for her.

WHAT DOES FOLLOWING A KING'S LEAD LOOK LIKE?

Let's be real with one another. Making our husband out to be the king in our home may not sound that appealing to a strong, intelligent, independent woman. So, let's approach this the way a queen would. I know that every woman reading this book has at some point longed for the lap of luxury where everything is roses and life is like a fairy tale. It's like that old commercial from when I was a child where the woman is stressed, the phone is ringing, the baby's crying, the dog's barking, dinner is burning, and someone is ringing the doorbell, all at the same time. Then she says, "Calgon, take me away!" and suddenly she's soaking in a beautiful bubble bath with soft music in the background and flower petals floating on the water. Her dreams come true and life has suddenly become a luxurious, warm *happily ever after*. We have all longed for that. To get there, we'll have to decide if we're willing to follow God's original design for the framework of marriage. In the end, that design gives us what we're all longing for, our power and purpose as a woman.

WHY DOES WHAT WE SAY MATTER?

Now, let me explain a few especially important points before going any farther. This information will help make some things more clear regarding translations and the original languages used in the Scriptures to define our role as husband and wife. The Bible is written in two parts, the Old and New Testament. The Old Testament was originally written in the Hebrew language, aside from a couple of passages in Aramaic. When Jesus spoke in the New Testament era, his native tongue was likely Aramaic since it had become the most common dialect at the time. When God began to call the authors of the New Testament to record his teachings around 50 to 100 A.D., they wrote the Scriptures in Greek since the Greeks had taken over as a world power. Thus, the Bible is primarily written in Hebrew in the Old Testament, and Greek in the New Testament.

If you've ever played the *Gossip Game* in school, you know how funny it is to see how miscommunication occurs. The first person whispers a message at the beginning of the game to the next person in line. As it's passed around the circle from person to person, the meaning is completely lost. The final words spoken at the end of the line rarely match the message spoken at the beginning. In fact, it rarely even comes close. It's typically hilarious when the two messages are compared. For example, you might start out saying, "The noble king rules his kingdom well." By the end of the game you might have, "T-Mobile rings my cell phone bell." When a message is passed from person to person, confusion can occur. Accordingly, anytime something is translated from one language to another, original meanings can be blurred, most likely because the tense and verbiage used in some dialects don't match the exact statement in another. As the Bible has been translated throughout history, official translators have determined not to change or alter the Bible's integrity. However, since most of us don't speak Hebrew or Greek, language barriers can sometimes occur.

Despite that barrier, the Bible's overall message remains steadfast. It is the inspired, inerrant, Holy Word of God. It records the impact of what God has done for us through the life, death, burial, and resurrection of Christ and that story has never changed. The teachings are the same; however, some meanings of words that God breathed into Scripture have lost their impact over time. That's why *submission* and *help meet* associated with marriage are such despised words by women in our culture today. Originally, these words weren't offensive to females since their meanings were clear and easier to understand in their original form. Between what we understand when we read them in English and what God really spoke when he inspired the authors many years ago, they can be slightly misunderstood. That means if we want to understand our role as royal rulers, we have to drown out the cultural voices of the day and replace them with the truth. To understand our identity as husband and wife, we must go back and look at what God first spoke in the original written languages of Hebrew and Greek.

WHAT DID GOD SAY AT THE FIRST WEDDING?

Now let's consider God's perspective at the point of creation when the first marriage took place. In Genesis 1:27 Moses wrote,

God created mankind in His image, in the image of God He created them; male and female He created them.

This means that both men and women were *equally* created to reflect God in who we are. As husband and wife, we're both made in the same image of the same God. In Galatians 3:28, again, equality is stressed when referring to our adoption.

There is neither Jew nor Greek, there is neither slave nor free, there is neither male nor female; for you are all one in Christ Jesus. (NKJV)

Neither is greater than the other as a son or daughter. From the very beginning, men and women were meant to be equals. We are equally loved and valued, but we are vastly different in design and destiny as we will see in this book. We were never meant to be the same or else there would be no reason for one of us to exist. Women and men are not the same scientifically in body or mind, and they're not the same in spirit as assigned to identity in marriage.

> *From the very beginning, men and women were meant to be equals. However, we were never meant to be the same.*

In 1 Timothy 2:13 we see that, "Man was created first" in the order of creation. We know God created Adam first, and then he took a rib from his side and created Eve. They were the first couple to enter into a marriage covenant, and God placed them in a luscious garden they called Eden. They lived, loved, and laughed freely throughout their paradise. The only stipulation given was not to touch the one tree in the middle of it all. Unfortunately, their carefree life began to unravel when Adam and Eve chose to disobey God on this issue. Sadly, it cost them their perfect marriage. In Chapter 1, we learned that it wasn't completely their fault thanks to the deception of the serpent, Satan.

WHAT LED SATAN TO DO HIS EVIL DEEDS?

Before Adam and Eve were created, God created the heavenly beings, or angels, to help him carry out the work in his kingdom. Satan was one of those beings and God made him one of the three archangels. He was a *commander* and a musician who radiated light and led worship. In other words, he led Heaven in worship from a highly regarded position in God's kingdom. One day he decided he wanted to be worshiped instead of lead worship. He determined to take over the kingdom and overthrow God from the throne. It was a heavenly coup d'état. As in the days of kings and castles, treason was underway, as the created tried to overthrow the Creator. Satan's attempt at mutiny was thwarted. It was an unforgivable act, and he was banished from the Kingdom. In medieval times, treason was punishable by death, but God, in his mercy, showed Satan more grace than any earthly king would have. He banished the enemy from Heaven versus demanding his life. Then he stripped him of his position, threw him out of His presence, and exiled him to the earth where he's been trying to rule ever since. We can see what happened in Isaiah 14:12-15, where God is speaking directly to Satan referring to him as the King of Babylonia.

King of Babylonia, you thought you were the bright morning star. But now you have fallen from heaven! You once brought nations down. But now you have been thrown down to the earth! You said in your heart, I will go up to heaven. I'll raise my throne above the stars of God. I'll sit as king on the mountain where the Gods meet. I'll set up my throne on the highest slopes of the sacred mountain. I will rise above the tops of the clouds. I'll make myself like the Most High God. But now you have been brought down to the grave. You have been thrown into the deepest part of the pit. (NIRV)

Satan knew he could never be restored to a right relationship with God because of what he'd done. Later when God placed the happy newlyweds in their lush oasis, he gave them the right to rule as king and queen over everything on earth. In Genesis 1:26.

God said, let us make man in our image, after our likeness. And let them have dominion over the fish of the sea, and over the fowl of the air, and over the live-stock, and over all the earth, and over every creeping thing that creeps upon the earth. (ESV)

In *The Message Bible* translation, it reads more poetically,

God blessed them: "Prosper! Reproduce! Fill (the) Earth! Take charge! Be responsible for fish in the sea and birds in the air, for every living thing that moves on the face of Earth".

Adam and Eve had full authority over his entire creation. The word *dominion* means "sovereign or supreme authority; the power of governing and controlling." Satan wanted the dominion they'd been given, so he could rule the earth instead, so he took on the form of a serpent, snuck into the garden, and sought to steal their reign. If he succeeded, he would steal the identity of all mankind. For that reason, he plotted and put his plan in motion. In Genesis 3:1, it tells us,

The serpent was craftier than any of the wild animals the Lord God made. He said to the woman, "Did God really say, 'You must not eat from any tree in the garden'"?

When Satan spoke, Eve listened. He convinced her to make the same mistake he'd made by creating a desire in her to be as *God*. First, he created doubt about God's motive for not allowing them to eat from the forbidden tree. Doubt about God is always an open door to wrong choices. Next, he convinced her if she took a bite she could be just like *God*. Sadly, she failed to understand the power God had already given her, and she fell for the enemy's deception. She ate from the tree and then offered Adam the chance to do the same. Eve thought the serpent was offering her a chance to trade for the best *Lily pad* in town with a throne. Instead, he was stilling her power and having her kicked out of the garden. At that moment, the perspective of men and women changed forever, and our identity and authority were lost as husband and wife.

Here's the good news! Jesus conquered the enemy's power over us by conquering evil as a sinless sacrifice on the cross. He then conquered death through his resurrection. Today we can be restored to our rightful place of authority through adoption and reclaim our right to rule the earth through Christ's power in our lives!

How did Adam and Eve's choices change our perspective?

Adam and Eve had lived in a luscious garden in perfect harmony with one another, without any problems or worries up to this point. There was no power struggle, no arguing, no apathy, and no conflict of any kind. They simply lived in perfect peace and loved one another completely. There was no chaos in their Caladiums, only peace in their Posies. Unfortunately, when they sinned, punishment was required. As with children and their parents, there are always consequences of wrong choices. Sadly, the consequences of their choices created chaos for us. As a result, a power struggle was birthed, and today husbands and wives both seek to dominate the other. Unless we choose to be adopted, we don't have the power to fully rule as husband and wife the way God originally designed. Sadly, our perspective has been shaped by the fall-out of their sin.

In Gen. 3:16b, God had these words to say to Eve for the consequence of her choice,

Your desire will be for your husband and (yet) he will rule over you.

Culturally, the word *desire* often refers to that of a sexual desire. However, in this Scripture the word is Hebrew and means "to control or to overtake." By putting the original meaning into the context of the verse, it went something like this when God spoke to Eve.

Your desire will be to control, overtake, or overthrow your husband, but your husband will rule over you instead.

Whew, take a deep breath! This means women everywhere struggle with their strong will to be in charge and take control of their kingdom. Women unknowingly seek to overthrow their husbands' position as king. This is where the root of the women's liberation movement (WLM) began. The seeds were planted in the Garden of Eden.

In today's world, the idea of a husband leading his home is relatively obscure due to the things we've been told for years about equality and women's rights. Let me be clear. Jesus and your Father God have always believed in equality and women's rights, but that's not what we've been told.

When examining the historical evidence, it becomes clear repeatedly in Scripture that Jesus stood up for the women in his life. He showed up and spoke up for the prostitute, the quadruple divorcee', the menopausal woman, the demon possessed woman, the widow, and the bride. God has never shortchanged the rights of women, yet many women are fighting for their right to be equal while criticizing God for limiting them in their design. This is simply a lie by the serpent.

WHAT DOES THIS EQUALITY MEAN?

Even though culture challenges us to rise up and take charge, the truth is, God's design has already given us charge as his daughter. We have the power to rule over the things in our area of dominion that God has purposed for us to rule. The key is to govern well, while maintaining our rightful position. Scripture clearly shows God created Adam first. This explains why we have an innate desire in our hearts for someone else to love us and lead us well. In our blueprint, God gave us incredible strength to succeed in the areas of leadership that clearly belong to us, while giving us the ability to follow in the areas that are not ours to rule. Unfortunately, most of us wrestle with following our husbands in the heat of the moment. Did you think you were the only one constantly battling with yourself to let your husband lead? I have some great news; you are not alone!

Despite being strong and powerful women, we all have an incredible need for our noble king to lead and protect us like a knight in shining armor while we consistently get in his way. Typically, after we've blown it and taken on authority in areas not ours to manage, we struggle with guilt and shame just like Adam and Eve did after they ate from the tree. We read in Scripture, they immediately gathered leaves to cover their bodies, and then they hid. They thought they were covering their nakedness, but they were really trying to cover their shame. Genesis 3:7b specifically says,

They sewed fig leaves together and made themselves aprons. (KJV)

They were ashamed because they failed at fulfilling their covenant in their role as husband and wife. Eve stepped out of her role by choosing to converse with a slimy serpent. Then she ate from the tree without conversing with the love of her life over a matter of importance. Adam, on the other hand, stepped out of his role as her protector by passively failing to guard her from the threat of a serpent's poison. The Scripture is clear, Adam stood, watched, and did nothing. They had been given everything they could ever need or want, yet it wasn't enough to motivate them to stay committed to the covenant of their marriage. If we're honest, we've all been there before. If you aren't married yet, you'll be there sometime in the future.

> Adam and Eve may have lost their right to govern, but we can take ours back and rule our kingdoms well.

Thank goodness, God wanted to fix their mistake and give us a second chance. He loved us enough to give us a *do over*. I don't think it's any coincidence that the curse on marriage given to Adam and Eve within Genesis 3:16 was completely reversed and redeemed by Jesus in the New Testament in John 3:16.

> *For this is how God loved the world: He gave His one only Son that everyone who believes in Him should not perish but have eternal life. (MOUNCE)*

God sent his son to die for the sin in the garden. He wanted to build that bridge to give us a way back to our original position as rulers. That's exciting news! Our new identity gives us the opportunity for marriage success. Adam and Eve may have lost their right to govern, but we can take ours back and rule our kingdom well!

CROWNING POINTS

- We have all been created to live in nobility
- Men and women are equals, but not the same
- Your desire to overthrow your husband is not your fault
- Things outside your design are not yours to reign
- You have dominion to rule the things only you can rule

Now that we've established how we got where we are, we can start considering where we're going. The remainder of this book is about *solutions* to the questions we have about our identity as a woman and wife. The answers can make our home more peaceful and less chaotic. Follow me as we put on the royal robe and learn together how to embrace solutions that will conquer the chaos!

SOLUTIONS

Chapter 5

WILL YOU PUT ON THE GARMENT OF PRAISE?

One of the most powerful things a woman holds in her hands is the ability to change any circumstance and make it beautiful despite how desperate it may seem. As we journey through the remainder of this book, we will address many aspects of whom we've been created to be as a woman. Those qualities are all equally important and yet different in nature. Overall, we can either choose to be the fragrance of peace or the aroma of hopelessness in any given crisis. What we choose to unleash is up to us. As a woman, we have the power to change, encourage, uplift, and calm down chaos when it comes. Scripture clearly states in Proverbs 31:15-16,

> *She is clothed with strength and dignity; she can laugh at the days to come. She speaks with wisdom, and faithful instruction is on her tongue.*

This passage states a woman is clothed in an admirable strength that allows her to bring humor into difficult situations. She can teach prophetically by releasing truthful words into her home that bring helpful, lifelong instruction. This means God created us to be not only daughters of the King but peace bearers to the palace.

Because of what Adam and Eve did in the garden, it unleashed warfare into our lives. The good news is, although our enemy may try to defeat us, he will never win! We can put our faith in that promise, bringing peace to our pandemonium. Based on our unique design, we're the one who sets the tone in our home. You've probably heard the saying, "If momma ain't happy, ain't nobody happy." Happiness is based on our peace and peace governs our perspective. Our perspective can persuade those around us to follow us into a place of peace or lead others into panic if we abandon the palace and head towards the castle when pandemonium comes.

HOW DO WE CONQUER THE CHAOS AND EMBRACE THE PEACE?

I think we can honestly say by this point we all prefer what the palace represents, but what happens when chaos comes knocking on the palace door without our permission? *Chaos* is a nation gone mad, a coronavirus unleashed, the loss of a job, the death of a loved one, a spouse who doesn't want the marriage you want, or even a child who walks away from everything you've raised them to believe. Reality is, one day *Chaos* will come knocking. How do I know? Because the Bible says so. There are many references to the fact we will face difficulties in our lives on this earth in the days to come. Psalms 34:19 warns,

> *Many are the afflictions of the righteous, but the Lord delivers him out of them all. (ESV)*

Here's the good news—*Chaos* is never an unannounced intruder to our Father. When turmoil bangs at the door, we can find peace in the promise that God already knew he was coming. More importantly, God will hand us the weapons we need on the threshold of war that we can cling to until victory comes.

When chaotic turmoil bangs at the door, we can find peace in the promise that God knew he was coming.

Throughout our thirty years together, Dan and I have faced a lot of chaos, some of which I've already shared. Each time, God was on time every time as the enemy banged at our palace door. One of our darkest hours came a year before our youngest son's birth. I awoke one morning to excruciating pain from a kidney stone. After the second ER visit where I felt like nobody was listening, I found myself in a life-threatening crisis. The stone was lodged causing my kidneys to fail and my body became sepsis. Sepsis is a serious bacterial infection in the bloodstream that causes organ failure. As Dan rushed me towards a cluster of downtown hospitals, he had no idea where to go. My cell phone rung, it was my closest friend who did not know what was happening except I'd had a stone diagnosed the day before. She had been praying for me that morning and heard the words "St. Joseph". She called to see how I was and what was going on. Dan explained, and they both knew St. Joseph's Hospital was where I needed to go. As I was admitted, doctors declared I might not make it through the night. While I was in ICU fighting for my life, Dan was in the hospital cafeteria begging God for his help. I had a team of about five doctors, but the most important doctor in my corner was the urologist. He had the least experience as a doctor, yet he turned out to be the physician that mattered the most. He surgically removed the stone and put in the stint to encourage my kidneys to work, but that's not what saved me. After several days in ICU, I had fought my way out of danger and was moved to a regular room.

Eventually, it started to seem the longer I stayed, the more new problems kept coming up. Each day was about a different organ. Rarely did anyone make it out alive with sepsis and the doctors had used experimental drugs to save my life. I was a phenomenon to them. On day seven, my urologist came by. He looked at me and said, "Mrs. White, the worst is over and you're going to make it, but I have to be honest. The longer you stay here the more at risk you become. You need to check yourself out of here and go home to get well." Later, as different doctors arrived announcing more tests and more drugs, I realized my urologist was right. That night as I lay all alone in my hospital bed, I made my way over to the window and pushed it open. Suddenly I felt a breeze rush in. I knew it was the breath of God. It was time to go home. The next day I refused the new panel of tests and demanded to be released. Dan was my knight in shining armor and rescued me and brought me home.

Just last year, I began to search for my urologist online. I wasn't sure why, but he had come to my mind many times since my illness. I wanted to thank him for saving my life. Because of his young age, it was doubtful he'd be retired. As I searched for him on the internet, I couldn't find him listed anywhere on his medical group's website. Then I typed his name into *google*. I was shocked when I saw his obituary. He had died not long after saving my life. I began to weep and worship. I realized God had been bringing my doctor to mind for a purpose. We were in a season of warfare for one of our children. God wanted me to understand that he is never too late when we're fighting for our lives or the lives of our children. The impact was in the revelation of the doctor's birthday listed on the obituary. Not only were we the same age, but he had been born just four days after me. The number *four* means "revelation" in scripture. I realized God knew *Chaos* was coming to my door bringing death on that day in that year. As he had stood and looked back over my life, he'd placed a weapon on my threshold that had saved me on death's door. That weapon was Dr. Kevin Reyes. The scripture tells us in Isaiah 46:10,

> *I declare the end from the beginning, and from long ago what is not yet done, saying; my plan will take place, and I will do all my will. (CSB)*

You and I can rest in the blessing of knowing God stands at the end of our lives and looks backwards to our beginning. Everywhere he sees the enemy coming, he puts a plan in place to give us victory. All we have to do is look, listen, and obey.

WHY DO BAD THINGS HAPPEN?

History shows the human struggle has been real from the beginning of time. There are three basic answers to why bad things happen. First, just like Adam and Eve, we can lose our paradise because of our own chaotic choices. Second, God might be allowing a test into our lives to strengthen our faith, knowing He'll give us the win in the end. Or, our chaos is an attack by the enemy of our soul who comes to rob, steal, kill and destroy us if he can.

No matter which of the three causes are the root of your chaos, the enemy of your soul seeks to use your circumstances to destroy your marriage. What Jesus came to redeem; he wants to demolish. Dan and I have learned from our experience that worship is an important key to our victory. When we find ourselves on the battlefield, we have to put on the garment of praise, suit up with the armor of God, and worship. Psalms 59:16 says,

> *But I will sing of your strength; I will sing aloud of your steadfast love in the morning. For you have been to me a fortress and a refuge in the day of my distress. (ESV)*

What does crisis do to a marriage?

In moments of chaos, warfare can undeniably take its toll on your love for each other. In our battles, there's been times when we rolled up our sleeves and fought together, and other times when we've put on our boxing gloves and clobbered each other. I can tell you from experience the first choice has always led to victory and the last has led to casualties of war. In reality, it's easier to fight and wound what we can see than defeat the villains that are invisible to the naked eye. God desires for us to join forces with him and defeat the enemy while we defend each other.

The first step to doing battle goes back to the saying I shared in Chapter 2. We have to know our enemy and know ourselves in order to win. We've learned a lot about our enemy, now let's learn more about ourselves. I can think of no better place to find that answer than from one of the greatest kings to have lived. King David put it this way in Psalm 149:14

> *I will praise you because I am fearfully and wonderfully made; your works are wonderful; I know that full well.*

It also states in Genesis 1:27 at the time of creation,

> *So, God created mankind in his own image; in his own image God created them; He created them male and female.*

Just as our Father is found in three parts as God the Father, Son, and Holy Spirit, he created the union of marriage the same way for the sake of strength. God often operates in what he calls a strand of three because of the power it holds. We'll dig into that a little more later. God not only wanted a husband and wife to become one with each other, he wanted us to become one with him. Shown in the diagram, as we grow closer to him, we automatically grow closer to one another.

He also designed the roles of Holy Matrimony to operate as a strand of three, mirroring the image of God. In that exquisite design, someone plays the role of the head of the home representing God. There's the role of Jesus, meant to be a servant leader ready to lay down his life if required. The final role is that of the Holy Spirit or the comforter. The mighty, rushing wind

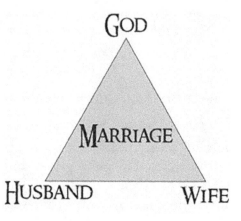

who moves throughout our lives shaking things up challenging us to greatness.

Ephesians 5:23 teaches that our husband was created to play the role of the head of the home, formed to be the noble leader who makes great decisions for his kingdom at large. He represents the Father who oversees the benefits and blessings of life just like God our Father does. He's charged with being our protector, using his unemotional wisdom to create strategic battle plans to defeat the enemy. Just as God provides, he's the main provider. That doesn't mean we can't have a career; it simply means our husband is the one held responsible for making sure every need in the kingdom is met. For that reason, God built within the nature of men the desire to labor and provide for those he loves. He's been wired that way naturally and God holds him accountable to his design.

The second role God gave our husbands is found in Ephesians 5:25 stating,

For husbands, this means love your wives, just as Christ loved the church. He gave up his life for her. (NLT)

This is the mandate calling our prince to be a marriage warrior. God holds them accountable for our safety and well-being, even if it means laying their life down in our place. Today, this idea seems to be offensive to so many women with them claiming they don't need the protection of any man. Remember God designed us to be powerful, so this idea is not meant as an insult. Rather, it should be viewed as God's way of loving us enough to send a warrior to fight on our behalf when we're under attack; the same way Dan fought for me in prayer as I was fighting for my life in intensive care. Men are called to a place of accountability for our overall safety, even if it means giving up and doing something they don't want to do. It means when we're in the middle of giving birth to

Woman is a magnificent gift of power given from the heart of God placed in the arms of man because he needs us.

their baby, they hold our hand and coach us through it. It means when we're sick, they feed us. It means when we lose our way in the chaos, they meet us where we are and carry us to safety.

WHO ARE YOU?

Hold on to your crown ladies, this might blow you away. The wife represents the powerful, uncontainable, ever moving Holy Spirit in the strand of three! In Scripture, the Holy Spirit represents the most power-ful force sent by God to empower man. Woman is a magnificent gift of power given from the heart of God placed in the arms of man because he needs us. Genesis 2:8 defines that,

It is not good for man to be alone.

Together we make up a tenacious strand of three, strong enough to withstand any formidable foe. Our husband's need us when they're in war. God knew this when he created this masterful three-part design. Together we form an undefeatable force against our enemy as we walk in the fullness of that design.

HOW DO I EMBRACE MY ROLE AS HOLY SPIRIT?

To embrace our identity fully as the representation of the Holy Spirit, we must put on the garment of praise because we set the tone for victory in the palace. In Bible times, God often sent out the worshipers before a battle. That concept has even carried over into our nation's history. If you've ever watched an historical battle reenactment, the Fife and Drum Corps march out first before a single shot is fired. Worship is the key to our triumph. 2 Chronicles 20:21 tells us,

> *When he had consulted with the people, he appointed those who sang to the Lord and those who praised him in holy attire as they went out before the army and said, "Give thanks to the Lord, for his loving kindness is everlasting."*

You may have heard the story of *David and Goliath* growing up. It's the story of a boy named David killing a giant. In the Old Testament, the prophet Samuel showed up unannounced and anointed David to become the future king of God's people when he was only a shepherd boy. He was a passionate worshiper, song writer, and warrior. He spent his life as a kid preparing for the future by leading a flock of sheep and worshiping God. His worship prepared him with the strength to rule once his throne arrived.

Young David's story unfolded when he went down to the battlefield carrying food for his older brothers who were soldiers in the Israelite army. When he arrived, he realized they were losing the war. In fact, they were hiding in their tents from the biggest, meanest Philistine as he taunted them from the valley below. He was a giant of a man named Goliath. David grew angry at the lack of action by the army and bravely stepped up volunteering to kill the mighty Philistine. Right before the battle, Saul, the king of Israel offered David his armor. David said "no" because it represented what the world had to offer him for protection. Instead, he chose to wear the only armor that fit his soul, a garment of praise. He stepped out with a slingshot and five stones and defeated the giant with one accurately slung rock powered by a whole lot of faith. His worship had made him a winning warrior. In Proverbs 18:21-22, we gain a greater understanding of this concept in our role as a wife,

> *Life and death are in the power of the tongue, and those who love it will eat its fruit. He who finds a wife finds a good thing and obtains favor from the Lord. (BSB)*

As a woman representing the Holy Spirit in our kingdom, what we speak holds the power and gives our husband victory from the Lord. When we worship the Father in Heaven, even if it appears we're losing on the battlefield, we change everything on the ground. Worship also makes the enemy tuck his tail and run. He can't stand hearing you sing your faith. Satan as we know was a heavenly worshiper until he turned his worship toward himself. Now he despises worship meant for the only God on the throne. We can use it to drive him away.

Over the last few years, as we've found ourselves in a different sort of war, God has used worship to encourage us. Often, I awaken each morning with a song playing in my head. I've learned from experience to look up the lyrics. Many times, I end up using the song during the day to stop a skirmish. As an added measure of weaponry at our palace, we play worship music softly twenty-four hours a day, seven days a week. When war is raging at the castle, we sing.

> *The very words we speak can either bring life to our situation or bring death to the circumstance.*

HOW DO I SUIT UP IN ARMOR?

With our garment of praise fully engaged, next we suit up in the armor God offers us for protection as listed in Ephesians 6,

> *Put on the whole armor of God, that you may be able to stand against the schemes of the devil... Therefore, take up the whole armor of God... Stand therefore, having fastened on the belt of truth, and having put on the breastplate of righteousness, and, as shoes for your feet, having put on the readiness given by the gospel of peace. In all circumstances take up the shield of faith, with which you can extinguish all the flaming darts of the evil one; and take the helmet of salvation, and the sword of the Spirit, which is the word of God... (ESV)*

The first five pieces are defensive in nature. They robe us in supernatural protection from our head to our toes, so let's start with the helmet of our salvation. It's the helmet of our identity in knowing our Abba Father as Lord and Savior and it keeps our thoughts clear during the fight. It straightens the crown on our head, giving us a sound mind as stated in 2 Timothy 1:7,

> For God has not given us a spirit of fear and timidity, but of power, love, and a sound mind. (KJV)

It means we fight by faith, not fear. When *Chaos* knocks, we stand firm on what looks like faith casting aside what acts like fear. Our natural inclination is to be afraid, which pushes us to grab for control and hold on to things that only God can hold. Our faith is counter to hanging on for dear life. It's letting go for the sake of finding the victory God has. When we surrender completely, his plans are fulfilled. Matthew 10:39 clarifies,

> If you cling to your life, you will lose it; but if you give up your life for me, you will find it. (NLT)

When we release our situation into his hands, he's more than able to make us conquerors. Victory starts with a clear understanding that we must put our faith in the one who is greater and walk into battle believing what he says.

Next, the breastplate of righteousness protects the heart and the other major organs from injury. We can't win without it because battlefields are full of heartbreak, grief, and shattered dreams. Wearing it means we exit the war with our hearts intact, despite the pain we experience. The breastplate falls into place when we get on our knees and ask the Father to unveil the places in our life that are unrighteous--the contributions we have made that invited *Chaos* to our home address. If the answer is truly "none", then we simply petition the Father to protect our heart and keep our motives pure as we help our husband fight. If we played some part, either directly or indirectly, then we confess it and ask for forgiveness. Then we stand up, free of guilt or shame, and forge ahead with our hearts protected.

Truth must surround us like a belt during battle, otherwise we could trip over our royal robe and fail to run the race. Without truth, we can fall prey to the voices in our midst instead of the Commander in Chief in our heart. When God sent my urologist to speak truth into my circumstance, he was handing me the belt of truth, so I could grab hold and run for the door. Our enemy is a liar. To defeat him, we must go into war with our eyes wide open, deciphering lies from truths as they blaze toward us like arrows. By ridding ourselves of untruths, we receive God's message clearly and march on.

If you're like me, you love shoes so this next piece of armor should be appealing. The shoes of peace are what we stand and run in on the battlefield. According to Scripture, they're tailored to our feet as a direct result of our salvation. Remember Cinderella? She was finally given her rightful position when she was fitted with the shoe only meant for her to wear. Miraculously, we can find peace in the middle of a war zone, while fiery darts of the enemy zoom past our heads, if we stand firm on God's promises. They are our peace. The battlefield becomes *Holy Ground* as we keep our eyes fixed on the Father instead of the chaos we see. This empowers us to walk in our beautiful glass slippers of peace even while the battle rages.

The last "defensive" piece of the armor meant to protect is the shield of our faith. Scripture says our faith is found in the things we hope for that God has promised, but we don't yet see. Historical data says that during ancient times it was normal practice for a soldier to have a shield created just for him based on his personal body measurements. That way, he could rest assured it would cover his entire body from head to toe. Romans 12:3 states,

> *For by the grace given to me I say to everyone among you not to think of himself more highly than he ought to think, but to think with sober judgment, each according to the measure of faith that God has assigned. (ESV)*

The shield of our faith has been measured unto us. It's believing for the things that seem impossible in the battle. It's found in the confidence of knowing our Father is who he says he is, and he will do what he says he will do. It's being sure of whom he truly is as Resurrected Savior, King of Kings, and Lord of all. In that faith, we can stand firm in the war and worship!

ARE PEOPLE OUR ENEMY?

Despite what you might think, our enemy is not the people in our present battle. Ephesians 6:12 teaches,

For our struggle is not against flesh and blood, but against the rulers, against the authorities, against the powers of this dark world and against the spiritual forces of evil in the heavenly realms.

We must keep in mind we are not fighting the people bringing chaos to our door. If we consider them our adversary, we will lose every time. They're casualties on the battlefield that the enemy is using against us. If we determine to destroy them out of bitterness or unforgiveness, the breastplate of righteousness falls off and the battle is lost. Instead, we pray for them out of compassion. Satan is our archenemy. Scripture says he's a roaring lion, roaming around seeking whom he can devour. Daniel, an Old Testament prophet of God, found himself thrown into a den full of ferocious lions. At that moment, Daniel chose to pray and not panic. God answered by sending angels to shut their mouths. The enemy's tactic is to roar loudly and drive us to fear, but if we listen to the battle cry of our Father's commands, our worship will silence the roar.

WHAT IS THE SIXTH PIECE OF THE ARMOR?

Finally, we're ready for the next piece of armor. Every other piece defends except for the sword. It is offensive. Notice this sixth item is something we hold in our hand. This means the war is still in our hands and God's hand is not yet in the battle. We'll grab hold of that weapon in the last chapter of the book. The Bible says the word of God is sharper than any two-edged sword. I believe one side of the sword is God's power and the other edge is our courage to speak his word out loud. Together they behead the lion.

Before beginning his ministry, Jesus entered the wilderness for forty days and nights where he faced Satan who had come to devour him. Jesus conquered him by wielding the sword of God's word. As the enemy offered him three tempting substitutes to the real thing God had planned, Jesus swung the sword of God's word and spoke it out loud defeating every lie. Speaking God's word in battle is also an act of worship. When we speak it, we're speaking his promises over the battlefield, so we can win the war.

In Jesus case, Satan had waited for him to enter the wilderness alone, not to mention hungry. Then he pounced with three tempting choices. First, he took advantage of his isolation. When chaos comes, it's natural to want to hide the truth from those around us out of embarrassment. I've learned from experience that hiding doesn't work, it only makes you more vulnerable. However, being honest and expressing personal struggles is a better option because it builds real life connections. It also opens doors for us to use our struggles to minister to others in the middle of theirs. Ministry helps us pull through and guards us from depression. I'm not encouraging an all-out radio announcement through the public broadcasting system, but don't be afraid to be honest with people you know you can trust about your personal war. They'll be your allies when you need prayer and encouragement. God has given us human connection to help us should we need it.

Next, the enemy offered Jesus food because he had not eaten in forty days. It was a substitute in exchange for the real bread of life. I think women struggle with this temptation the most. I've found myself on a battlefield, tempted to grab food for comfort. Satan offered food to Jesus in hopes of taking advantage of his vulnerability. Jesus reminded him he did not live by bread alone but by God's word. If we're not careful, we can grab for food when what we need most for nourishment is God's word over our calamity. Winning doesn't involve sitting down at the table and using food to soothe our pain. We've got to reach for the only substance that can fill the emptiness in our gut. The Scripture will sustain us and destroy the enemy's substitutes. We win by living on and digging into the bread of life to sharpen our sword. Then we speak it out loud when the enemy comes.

Next, Satan offered Jesus the chance to rule a false kingdom instead of the whole world. We can't accept anything less than the victory God has to offer. Don't allow yourself to accept the substitute of a short-term win versus a long-term, bigger defeat of your adversary. The battle may be long, but God's grace will sustain you. Run the race before you and you'll reach the finish line.

Lastly, Satan offered Jesus the opportunity to prove his strength by jumping from a tower versus hanging on a cross. Jesus chose the most painful option because winning a war requires sacrifice. Something has to die. We may have to sacrifice our pride, our goals, or even our dreams to win. Anything we grasp and hold to that God is asking us to release must be laid at the cross, so we can pick up the sword and possess life in the end. Winning might mean moving. It might mean changing jobs, or churches. If you know the Commander in Chief is calling you to sacrifice something in the war, you can rest assured he'll use it to help you win and resurrect your future.

We all want a peaceful palace, but when chaos comes knocking at our door, we can put on the full armor and take hold of the sword and worship until victory comes!

CROWNING POINTS

- Straighten your Crown, the thoughts in your head matter
- Protect your heart and fasten your belt
- Slip on the shoes of peace meant for only you
- Hold up your shield and speak God's word out loud
- Have your partners back, he needs you
- Put on a garment of praise and worship your way to victory

God holds your victory in his hands, but we want to help. If you need someone to pray for your circumstances, reach out to us at www.ChaosOrPeace.us. The keys to winning in battle are knowing who you are, knowing who your enemy is, and walking in complete faith in the God who has already won the war! Now let's move forward and learn what it means to help the king of our heart.

Chapter 6

WILL YOU HELP THE KING?

God's intent when he created Adam and Eve was for them to be his hands and feet on the earth and enforce his will and defeat the enemy. From the beginning, he designed the role that each spouse would play to make us more powerful together. The first title given to Eve was that of help meet. The modern-day term often used is *helpmate*. This term only refers to "companionship between partners". Whereas, *help meet* in the original language refers to "a relationship between a husband and wife." I'll be using the term *help meet* due to its significance in relation to marriage.

From the minute Eve arrived on the scene, being Adam's helper was her first mandate. Her established role six-thousand years ago was designed to bring revelation to our role today. As stated in Scripture, when Adam realized all the other living creatures had mates, he suddenly became aware of his aloneness. God then created Eve to fulfill the role of woman to be his helper. Many women have falsely come to believe that being a man's helper sounds a lot like being called a king's servant. This is not at all what our role is, and it's not the beautiful picture God had in mind when he designed us and called us "*help meet.*" In fact, it's almost the opposite of what you might be thinking. Scripture declares in Genesis 2:18,

And the Lord God said it is not good that the man should be alone; I will make him a help meet for him. (KJV)

Before we can embrace this title, we must first understand it. The word *help* in Hebrew is *ezer* which means "to help." It's also pronounced *azar* which means "to surround, protect, and aid." In the second part of the word, *meet* is pronounced *kenegdo* in Hebrew which means "corresponding to, counterpart to, equal to, and matching." When the two words are combined, we gain new perspective on our design which many of us have never heard. God was saying he created woman to surround man with her love, protect him with her body, help him with his life, and walk beside him as his equal partner. He never intended us to be a *maid* in a subservient role. Being married doesn't get any better than God's description of a help meet!

In this chapter, I'll share the nuts and bolts of how you and I can fulfill that role as stated in Genesis 2:18. I hope these examples stimulate your imagination. Every marriage is different. The dynamics of every couple varies. Your strengths and his weaknesses will differ from the ones my husband and I share. Your goal as you read this chapter is to let your imagination run wild with ideas and ways you might be able to help the king by your side. Even though every couple is different, some dynamics of how females and males relate are the same. Other than that, your role as help meet will evolve based on your personal relationship with one another. Hopefully, this chapter will help promote your success as queen of the palace and helper to the king. Let's get started!

ARE YOU A DIAMOND IN THE ROUGH?

Proverbs 12:4 proclaims,

A wife of noble character is her husband's crown, but a disgraceful wife is like decay in his bones.

According to this verse, we have two choices when it comes to being a beautiful tiara, and both are stated in this Scripture. If we choose to be a help meet, we can actually be our husband's priceless crown! A *crown* is defined in the dictionary as "an ornamental circlet or head covering, often made of precious metal set with jewels and worn as a symbol of sovereignty." The definition of *sovereignty* is "supreme power,

authority, rule, and dominion." Can you see it all coming together? We are the crown atop our husband's head, and the crown gives us both dominion over the earth that God established at creation.

If we choose to be a help meet, we can actually be our husband's priceless crown!

Let's explore what the symbol of the crown means to the king of any kingdom. In the days of kings and queens and coronations, the relevance of the crown on the king's head was not just about the crown itself. It represented the stamp of approval for noble leadership marking his full authority over the kingdom. The crown held all the glory of what his leadership would mean. It was always presented at a formal coronation service. If you think about it, we were similarly presented to our husbands at the beginning of our wedding service. Our wedding was our husband's formal coronation! Back then, the ceremony was full of traditions and guidelines held to extreme importance. If something went wrong, they believed it could jinx the king and his rule over the kingdom. If we're the crown and our husband's glory, we hold the key to promoting his authority and dominion, so he can succeed as a leader. Understanding this part of our role is especially important. We don't want to destroy our husband's ability to rule the kingdom and cause his crown to topple to the ground and fall apart. Behind every good man is a great wife, and on the head of every great king is a beautiful crown. God has given us an incredible position as women. As we will learn in the next chapter, even though we're equals, by placing ourselves underneath our husband in rank and order, we're elevated to the top of his head to crown him with our beauty.

WHAT'S IN A CROWN?

Let's consider the beauty of the crown for a moment. If you've ever had the privilege of seeing a real crown full of diamonds, they are spectacular! If not, I want to challenge you to go out on the internet and search for some of the world's most beautiful tiaras. They're stunning. I happen to think diamonds are a girl's best friend because we were originally designed to be a priceless jewel ourselves. They represent everything beautiful and captivating within us. For one of our anniversary trips, Dan and I were fortunate enough to take a trip to Europe where we visited the Jewel House at the Tower of London. It's where the crown jewels of the royal family are on display. They were the most beautiful pieces of royal history we'd ever seen. As I started writing this chapter, I reflected on that trip and drew some parallels between those jewels and our role as help meet.

First, I considered how the jewels are protected underneath unbreakable glass cases because they are priceless, precious heirlooms. They're irreplaceable as symbols of the royal family heritage. The glass cases protect them from dust and fingerprints, so they don't lose their luster. They guard them from the possibility of thieves trying to steal them or remove valuable pieces from their mounts. Let's consider how God gave Adam a mandate to protect Eve. In symbolism, God created our husband to be the glass case over our life. In proper rank and order, we are protected underneath them. God did not place us there because we're weak, but because we have immeasurable worth. He considered woman priceless and irreplaceable. God knew we would help build the family heritage by birthing the next generation of warriors. Through our sentimental, feminine nature we breathe life into the kingdom.

God called man to protect woman, because just like the jewels in London, there is no substitute for a beautiful woman. No one else holds the power to help the king. No one else can birth the heirs to the throne, and no one else can nurture them to become the next generation of leaders. For this reason, our Creator commanded the husband to nobly defend and preserve the exquisite life of the wife just as the glass cases safeguarded the crown jewels.

ARE CROWNS AS FRAGILE AS THEY SEEM?

As we viewed the family gemstones, I realized they're not as fragile as you would imagine. They're well-made with precise detail and pristine craftsmanship, establishing them as some of the most priceless jewels in the world. As King David, proclaimed to our Creator in Psalms 139:14,

Thank you for making me so wonderfully complex! Your workmanship is marvelous—how well I know it. (NLT)

As stated in this verse, we too are made wonderfully complex by the hands of God. We're priceless, beautiful jewels. Handcrafted by our Creator with great care and concern, so we can fulfill our glorious purpose. There's nothing like the beauty of a woman.

I remember thinking while at the jewel house, "What would happen if the jewels were stolen?" I even pondered why the royal family would choose to take that risk by putting them on display for the world to see. Now I realize they afforded us the opportunity because their beauty demanded it. The royal family chose to share them instead of hiding them away in a vault because their exquisite virtue earned them the right to be seen. As wives, we don't need to be placed in a subservient role isolated from the rest of the world. When we're walking in our role as help meet, we deserve to be elevated in freedom. We're to be admired and esteemed by the world as we radiate the beauty of our design. As a crown of glory, we can lead other women to desire that same value for themselves. We represent the *crème de la crème* of what our husband holds dear. When we glow in the radiance of our identity, it gives us the freedom to shape and influence culture in a positive way. There's nothing more enchanting than a man with a captivating *help meet* in all her radiance crowning his head with glory.

AS A CROWN OF GLORY, WHAT WILL YOU REFLECT?

It was mid-afternoon as the sunlight came piercing through the windows in full radiance at the Tower of London. The thing I remembered most was the glow the gemstones created in the room. The brilliance they reflected was almost blinding as they performed their own magnificent light show on the surrounding walls. In the Bible, God is referred to as the *light of the world* and the *bright and morning star*. When he pours his love out on us through our husbands in a marriage relationship, we become a reflection of God's light to the world. Like crown jewels, we take our rightful position in all our radiance and undeniably become our husband's crown. We were created to be the glory on his head as he walks out the role of being the king in our home.

How do we become our husband's crown?

In both the Old and New Testament, the word *glory* was used to speak of "great honor, praise, value, wonder, and splendor." In 1 Corinthians 11:7 we find the mandate given to both man and woman about glory.

> *A man ought not to cover his head, since he is the image and glory of God; but woman is the glory of man.*

You might be asking, "Why should a man not cover his head and what does it mean to glorify man?" Our husbands need no other covering but the glory of a wife who exemplifies respect, honor, and nobility. We glorify our husband by rising up and stepping into our position as the headdress in his life. The Webster's Dictionary defines the word *helper* as "someone who works to make things better or easier for someone else, to assist, aid, and to support." We could substitute the word *love* in place of *helper* because "to help" is love in action. It's something we committed to in our vows, "to love and to cherish". Out of love for our husband and our Father, we can make our husband's life better and easier by assisting and supporting him. As a result, he becomes everything he was created to be. When everyone's walking in their designated identity, both husband and wife are set in motion to intersect their destiny. If I help him become what he was created to be, I become what I was created to be. I don't know about you, but I want to be the beautiful diamond tiara God designed me to be.

What does a help meet do?

There's an example in the Old Testament of a woman named Ruth. Her love story is one of tragedy and triumph. Ruth was widowed at a young age, and back in her day when your husband died, the closest single next of kin stepped up to rescue the widow from poverty and vulnerability. He was called the *kinsman redeemer* defined as "the man called to marry a widow to take her husband's place." His role was to produce an heir for the man who died. Feelings of love in this scenario didn't usually have any part in the story. It wasn't based on emotion but practicality. For Ruth, the possibility of a *redeemer* seemed hopeless.

She found herself all alone in a strange land taking care of Naomi, her mother-in-law, who was also a widow. God saw Ruth's need and her potential as well as her sacrifice to help another widow in need, and he worked a miracle on her behalf.

This beautiful storyline unfolds as Boaz, her deceased husband's next of kin, falls in love with her. It was the tradition of widows to forage for food in grain fields until they were redeemed. As the sweat glowed on her brow, Boaz the owner of the field was captivated by her beauty. To keep from starving, she walked behind the field hands looking for grain they dropped during harvest. Boaz had heard about Ruth and was impressed by her willingness to care for Naomi. He told his laborers to leave behind extra grain for her to find. One night, on the advice of Naomi, Ruth made herself beautiful and went to lay at the feet of Boaz as he slept. In those days, this was an act of humility done in hopes of becoming their servant. By embracing her circumstances, she gained more than she imagined. As a result of her humility, hard work, and her generosity to care for Naomi, Boaz fell in love and took her as his bride. Instead of becoming a servant, she became the wife of a wealthy farmer. Instead of begging for food, she had more than enough to eat. Instead of becoming a slave, she became her husband's crown and glory. She was married and redeemed by a kinsman, not out of duty but out of love. The qualities she exhibited won the heart of her king, and we can learn a lot from her example.

Ruth gathered and gleaned in the field without worrying about her future. She could have abandoned Naomi, but she chose to remain loyal instead. We, too, can choose to walk in our role and care for our family as loving nurturers. We can remain loyal and committed instead of abandoning our post. In this fast-paced world of technology, mothers and wives are abandoning real relationships for the sake of impersonal connections. Social media will never return the love we're looking for, but the relationships in our home will. We can gather and glean in our field of harvest with our intuitive nature just like Ruth. We can make sacrifice to nurture those under our care. We can also walk in humility while embracing who we are in our design. These are the character traits of a help meet. By gathering information in our homes as our field of harvest, we can captivate the heart of our kinsman redeemer. Jesus is our Heavenly Kinsman Redeemer and in his love for us, he sent us an earthly redeemer by giving us the opportunity to marry. He gave us a husband who could love, honor, and protect us until his return like the glass case over the crown jewels in London. Living out the *Ruth* principle of gathering, gleaning, and giving, helps us aid, support and assist our husbands by making their life easier.

HOW DO WE GATHER, GLEAN, AND GIVE INFORMATION?

Just as Boaz fell in love with Ruth while she gathered and gleaned, we can capture our husband's heart by gathering and gleaning the details and events going on around our palace while using the gift of intuition. *Intuition* is defined as "the ability to understand something immediately from instinctive feeling without the need for conscious reasoning, inner sensing, or inner insight". Female intuition is woven into our very nature. It started at creation when God took a rib from Adam's side to create Eve. The rib cage is intended to be the protector of all the vital organs. One of the main organs it protects is the heart. If you've ever wondered why you're typically the first one in the palace to notice when something's wrong, it's because you were created to notice the details. As a wife, you'll notice when your marriage relationship may be strained or if you and your spouse seem to be drifting apart. You might even intuitively know if he has a physical condition that needs a doctor's attention. If you have children, you're the one in the home that notices when a child seems sad or needs to talk. Being in touch with the heartbeat of the home means you're always in touch with what's going on and the emotional side of the relationships in your kingdom. This is how we gather information as the Holy Spirit!

The definition of *gleaning* is "to gather bit by bit" as Ruth did. We gather information one question at a time, one piece at a time, one day at a time. It comes natural for us to ask lots of questions. If we're feeling an emotional vibe about something, we start investigating. I'm sure your husband has already noticed this fact. We might ask him for the details about a phone conversation, how a meeting went at work, or what's bothering him. We might ask our children how their day was at school, or why the sad face. All of these actions, God meant for us as help meet.

If we're going to be in touch with the heart of the matter, we must glean the details and relay that information to our husband for their leadership and resolution. If you work outside the home, you can still fulfill your role as a noble queen. Despite not being home every day, that special quality of female intuition will still be a part of your *help meet* responsibility. You may have to work a little harder to catch up, but your role never changes. Despite our careers, it's still our responsibility to notice the heart of what matters at the palace and share those details with our husband if there's a problem.

> —◦◦◦—
> *Our job as help meet is to gather, glean, and give information to win the war for our homes.*
> —◦◦◦—

If you've been married for long, you've probably noticed men are not naturally intuitive at all. They just want the facts. It's not a flaw in their design; it's what gives them incredible strength in a time of crisis to make great decisions. It enables our husband to draw up the battle plan with a less emotional perspective, so we can all win. Our job as help meet is to gather, glean, and give information to help our husband win the war for our home.

HOW DOES THIS LOOK ON A DAILY BASIS?

Here are practical ways you and I can be our husband's help meet without doing a hostile takeover and overthrowing the throne. Through the years, I've done different things depending on Dan's need at the time. In the early days, if I knew the lawn needed mowing, which was *his* territory, I might surprise him and *just do it*! Then we had more time together after his long day at the office. Another example might be as simple as gathering information about purchases or services we needed and giving it to him to help in the decision-making process. Here's an example. Every time we've moved, I gathered the names of companies, their phone numbers, days of service, and pricing for garbage pickup. Dan took that information and made the decision. I did the same thing regarding home and car insurance companies, their quotes, services and payment plans, as well as how they were ranked nationally to other companies. I then passed it along with my input, and he made the decision. I was helping make his life easier by saving him a lot of time he didn't have. Our role to gather, glean, and give is a plan I call the G^3 *War Strategy.*

> ❖ Gather: to intuitively observe and seek answers.
> ❖ Glean: to gather bit by bit one question at a time, one day at a time.
> ❖ Give: to lay what you have gathered and gleaned at the feet of your husband, so he can use the intel to formulate a plan and win the war.

Many women struggle with this concept because of our desire to overthrow. It's in our nature to want to be the one making decisions. In reality, we are helping make decisions, by gathering and gleaning the information they need. In the next chapter we'll examine your husband's A^5 War Strategy and how the two strategies work together so you and your husband can successfully command the army under your watch.

This plan is an important aspect to our marriage success. By being our husband's help meet, he can be the best leader and father he can be. As a wife and mother, we keep our husband informed, so he can command the kingdom underneath our care.

How do children fit into to this model?

The process is the same once children arrive. A mother is constantly looking at what's going on in the hearts of her children. We are more emotionally in touch with their actions, especially if we're home or in contact with day-care providers or schoolteachers. If we see a child struggling, we give that information to our husband following the G^3 War strategy. Then he simply follows the A^5 War Strategy and provides a plan to defeat the enemy.

In this model, our children are our troops. They're in training learning how to defeat their enemy as adults. In the same way, a sergeant would present the general to the soldiers in his regiment, we present our husband as someone to be revered by our children. How he's viewed will determine his success in leadership. Image is everything in a kingdom. When our children were younger, I remember leading them to surprise Dan by standing at the back door waiting to cover him in hugs and kisses as he arrived home from work. Once for fun, we got on our knees and shouted, "Welcome home, king of the palace!" This seems so simple and maybe even silly, but the truth is, it turns their hearts toward their father with admiration and respect. Now that they're older, they still see him through those same eyes. All of this is a part of keeping their hearts loyal to their leader. That loyalty transfers over to keeping their hearts loyal to God their Father and his leadership in their lives as adults.

HOW CAN I HELP WITH HIS CAREER?

You and I may also be able to play a part in helping our husband in their professional success, if not in a direct way, in an indirect way through prayer and support. It's important to know what's going on in our husband's life and especially his career. It's imperative to show interest in what he's passionate about. In the early part of our marriage, Dan was an electrical engineer and used his skills as an inventor for his corporation. He was responsible for new ideas relating to cash registers, known as *point of sale terminals*. Since I did most of the shopping for our family, I made it a point to be on the lookout for problems that arose while paying for purchases, especially if the store used the product my husband designed. If I ran into an issue while checking out, I questioned the check-out staff for their opinion. I was gathering and gleaning information to help Dan be the best at what he already did well. He then took the information and used it to enhance his company's products. He even used it to create new inventions if needed. It was my way of contributing to and showing him thanks for all he did to provide for our needs. He's been privileged to receive many patents for his innovative ideas, and I like to think I've played some part in helping him hang his twenty-four patents on our palace walls.

I do want to give a word of advice about stepping slowly into this role unless you understand your husband's career fully. He has to be completely comfortable with your input. After coming up with some helpful ideas of your own, I suggest you discuss those with your husband and allow him to express some areas where he could really use your help. By doing so, you run less of a risk of overstepping your boundaries. As you begin to understand how you complement your husband in his job, you can be a more powerful help meet. Let me caution you about one issue we've faced. I've learned the hard way that making comments about something I don't like about an unfair decision at his corporation or maybe a new boss is not helpful at all. Instead of looking like I'm defending him, it comes across as not being supportive. Support in the areas you can and leave the realities of his situation up to him.

There may be some things you discover by trial and error. When that occurs, make a mental note of the areas to avoid and don't offer advice there unless he specifically asks. Just knowing and showing interest in what your husband does can be a great encouragement to him. Helping him succeed can be as simple as keeping it quiet around the house if he works from home. In our design to help, how we help can change with the seasons of life. For example, after our third child was born, sleep deprivation was a nightly occurrence. That meant when Dan left for work, I was usually sound asleep. During that season, I tried to make sure there were plenty of fast and easy options for him to eat for breakfast, and he knew where to find them. Later, when the kids and I would eat breakfast, I might even make extra for him to heat and have the next morning. Now, Dan is in sales where he's selling many of the things he helped invent. As a result, my role has changed. Praying for favor, success, and prosperity in his sales, and safety as he travels, is how I help him the most. Depending on where you are, you may have to adjust how you contribute at different times but help from a queen's heart will usually always be appreciated.

Since our husbands all have different job descriptions, it will require some thinking on your part as you put together ideas on ways you can help your knight in shining armor succeed. Life changes all the time, but the possibilities of helping him are limitless. When he is winning as a leader at home and in his career, so are you!

CROWNING POINTS

- You can choose to be your husband's crown of glory
- You were not created to rule things outside your domain
- Lifting him up with encouragement, elevates you to your position
- A crown is the most powerful position a queen can hold
- As you shine in your role, he steps into his role as king

Now that we've learned how to become our husband's crown and glory, we can move forward to receive our marching orders. Follow me as we begin to learn how to march in rank and order!

Chapter 7

WILL YOU FOLLOW RANK AND ORDER?

Now that we've established and defined our identity as *help meet* and clothed ourselves in the armor of praise, let's explore what our war strategy looks like as we march in rank and order. This concept will allow us to take our place on the throne in our home and fully embrace our husband on the battlefield.

First, let's clarify who is ranked in what order. God is clearly ranked above humans as our Creator. We don't just answer to each other in marriage, we answer to the one who created man and woman for the covenant of marriage. Just as we are under the authority of our earthly father, or the person who raised us, we answer to our Heavenly Father who created us because we are his children called to be in relationship with Him. In battle, he's our Commander in Chief.

As mentioned, marriage was the first relationship God established between humans. You may ask yourself why God created marriage. He established that it was not good for man to be alone as stated in Genesis 2:18. To reveal Adam's need, God told him to do a zoo review and name all the animals of creation along with their mates. As a result, Adam realized there was no companion for him. In his love for Adam, and in following through with God's original plan to create everything to reproduce itself, God designed a mate just for him as his lifelong companion. God established this relationship not only for companionship but to help them both become better as individuals. Marriage isn't meant to be easy; it's meant to mold us and shape us by challenging us to become less selfish and more loving. It's a relationship created to refine us almost like sandpaper refines a rough piece of wood. If Adam had remained alone there would have been no motivation for him to become the best person he could be. God recognized our human need for change.

WHAT IS THE BIGGER PICTURE?

There's another reason God created marriage. It was for the bigger plan. Our covenant is the picture we paint together to reflect God's image to the world. Isaiah 62:5 is one example,

As a young man marries a young woman, so will your Builder (Jesus) marry you; as a bridegroom rejoices over his bride, so will your God rejoice over you.

Here the prophet Isaiah clearly calls us the bride and Jesus the groom in his scriptural writings. In context, God used the image of marriage because it was something he knew the people would understand, but he also wanted to define our perspective. God intended for marriage on earth to clearly be the personification or tangible picture of his followers in a covenant relationship to Jesus in Heaven. When we marry our spouse, we have the awesome opportunity of living out that illustration for others to see. Our marriage to each other can reveal who Christ is to the world as a visible, living example. If we do it well, others will not only consider the beauty of a healthy marriage relationship, but also be drawn to learn more about how we make marriage work. We get to share with them the method of our success, and they get to learn more about Jesus who can then draw them toward a covenant relationship with him. This is the bigger picture we were created to paint for the world to see!

Sadly, because so many couples are living in castles of chaos versus palaces full of peace, that image isn't really catching on. In fact, evidence clearly shows more and more couples have no desire to marry. It's also clear many have no desire to know who Christ is since marriage has become such a revolving door. People all around us are missing out on knowing God's love because we're doing such poor job of loving each other.

WHAT IS A STRAND OF THREE?

I believe we can shift the trends of our culture away from abandoning marriage. Scripture clarifies, "nothing is impossible with God." To do this, we must start by strengthening our own marriage to fortify the walls of the kingdom. Our kingdom's fortification comes from the Lord and his covering above us and walls of protection around us. If we accept his adoption by faith, he becomes the protective strand that binds our hearts together in a triune relationship. In Ecclesiastes 4:12, King Solomon asserts,

Though one may be overpowered, two can defend themselves. (But) a cord of three strands is not quickly broken.

This confirms why Adam was never meant to be without a mate. God knew alone he could easily be overpowered. Together Adam and Eve could defend themselves, but with God's presence woven into their lives the bond would not easily be broken. God would serve as a buttress for their protection. As we already know, marriage is a triune relationship formed in the image of a triune God and our relationship is a strand of three. The verse above makes this concept more powerful.

The idea of the three strands is exactly why most ropes are made as triple cords woven together in some form or fashion. Rope-making dates back to the Egyptians in 2000 BC. Even though technology and materials might have changed over time, the way ropes are made hasn't changed at all. The woven three stranded rope is how the Israelite slaves moved massive stones to build the great pyramids in Egypt. Today, rope is used around the world to perform many forceful tasks. One such example is on U.S. Navy ships, where rope is used from the smallest to the largest tasks in a war. As stated in an old *Navy Cadet Handbook*, no longer in print, the Navy's larger ropes are made up of three stranded ropes woven together in multiples of three. In human logic it would seem the more strands the stronger the rope. However, the Navy states that studies have shown a two stranded rope breaks too easily, and a rope made of four is weaker overall.

I caught a firsthand glimpse of this Scripture and the strength of three stranded ropes early in our marriage. Dan and I found ourselves needing to bring down an oak tree about one-hundred feet tall weighing in at over a thousand pounds. There was no money in the budget to pay a professional tree removal company, and we were too naive to know better. We determined to do it ourselves regardless of our lack of experience. With a chain saw, a rope, and a whole lot of determination, we attempted our hand as lumberjacks.

> With the strength of three strands added to sheer determination, a married couple can conquer almost any giant.

It wasn't until I saw the rope Dan had bought that I got a little concerned. I'd pictured a big thick rope like you see in a tug of war game, but instead he brought out this small white rope about the size of my ring finger. He assured me it would work because the package stated the weight it could bear before breaking. It was more than the weight of our tree. Dan did the cutting and I did the tugging. I learned the lesson of my life that day about the strength of three strands. As I found myself running for my life to get out of its path, the tree came crashing down. I realized then that with the strength of three strands added to sheer determination, a married couple can conquer almost any giant in their life.

WHY IS A STRAND OF FOUR A BAD IDEA?

We can learn from other couples about the weakness created in a strand of two and a strand of four. As we've already established, the enemy has been weaving himself into relationships since the Garden of Eden. God was meant to be the tie to bind Adam and Eve's hearts together, but when Satan slithered into the garden and wrapped himself around a tree, the presence of a fourth member in the human relationship was added and the strand of three began to unravel. Their marriage had become a strand of four. Abraham and Sarah were another couple who made this huge mistake, and we'll learn more about their story later.

The weakness of a strand of two causes relationships to easily break. We can see those relationships all around us as couples try to forge their forever love story but never stop to consider where they will draw their strength. When the storms blow in, their house comes tumbling down because a strand of two easily breaks. In the middle of our seven-year journey through my father's estate, Dan and I had nothing to give one another. Had there not been a third strand present with God woven into our story, our marriage would have unraveled.

If we're going to succeed at Holy Matrimony, we must realize the importance of God binding our marriage together while refusing to allow any other strand into our covenant. He has to become the King of our hearts and the fortress of our protection. The strand of three in a relationship between husband and wife has always been the best choice for marriage. With our Father intertwined throughout our bond, we can do marriage in his strength and not our own. That idea alone makes it easier as a woman to establish our husband as the king of our home according to God's design in rank and order.

Following a husband is not popular with the majority of women we know and the female population at large. I have to be frank; the terms of *help meet* and *submission* weren't appealing to me either. When Dan and I first married, I'd get a chill up my spine at the word pictures they created. I felt the same way as most women until I began to grasp what rank and order really meant. Primarily my opinion of what a wife's role looked like was based on the same lie the Serpent originally told Eve. He convinced her she could be in charge like God if she ate the fruit from the tree of knowledge. More importantly, he implied that if she didn't take charge, she was somehow inferior. He is a liar. Following our rank gives us the power to be the woman we've been created to be and put our home in order.

FOLLOWING RANK AND ORDER = POWER AND PURPOSE

Women are extraordinarily strong. If we're honest, we might even say we're *strong-willed*. Eve was strong-willed, so we come by it naturally. The good news is our strong-willed strength doesn't have to be a negative attribute! Once we begin to understand the role we were designed for, we can embrace the strength we possess in a healthy way. I found incredible freedom by walking in determination as a wife without it hurting my marriage. God created us with strength, so we could accomplish great things. In fact, by walking out marriage in the proper rank and order, we win the war while standing bravely beside our warrior on the battlefield.

CAN YOU GIVE ME AN EXAMPLE?

For many years we've been told by magazines, books, television, and even other women that if we don't take charge and command our independence, we are somehow weak, or we'll never reach our potential. We've been raised to believe that a *real* woman would never submit to her husband's authority. This is the same lie Satan told Eve, "Don't submit, just indulge, and you will be in charge like God." God did not create us to be inferior to our husbands at all. As I've mentioned, the Scriptures teach "all men and women were created equal." We're all created in His image for His purpose. To understand the weight of this, let's gather more insight.

God, Jesus, and the Holy Spirit are considered complete equals. Christ was the flesh form of God. Christ came to earth in human form and willingly chose to place himself underneath God's authority. It was the choice he made to carry out the beautiful plan to redeem mankind. He wasn't forced into submission; it was clearly his decision. He often said, "I came to do what my Father has sent me to do."

Choosing to put himself under God's authority did not make him inferior to the Heavenly Father. Instead, it freed him up and gave him complete power to fulfill his purpose and reach his destiny. When we understand this, we can willingly place ourselves underneath our husband's leadership. This allows us to carry out God's beautiful plan to redeem our marriage and family. Choosing to walk in our role frees us up and propels us into our full potential!

Honestly as a wife, one of my greatest battles has been dying to my independence. I'm a very capable person. Most of my life I've lived by the motto, "Where there's a will there's a way!". I know how to take charge and get things done. However, when I recognized I was in a battle for my marriage, with my children's best interest at heart, I realized that I needed to examine myself. My tendency to live by that motto can cost me the victory and harm those around me who are watching. In a real war, if a sergeant takes the same authority over his general, I've taken over my husband at times, it could cost him the lives of his soldiers and the war.

WHAT IS RANK AND ORDER?

Paul, a great preacher and teacher back in the first century, wrote about marriage in the New Testament. He had a lot to say about the role of husbands and wives. He wrote in Ephesians 5:22, 24,

Wives be subject to your own husbands, as to the Lord. But as the church is subject to Christ, so also the wives ought to be subject to their husbands in everything. (NASB)

What does *be subject to* mean? Let's look at its original definition. The word *subject* is a Greek term *hupotasso*. It's a military term meaning "to arrange in a military fashion under the command of a leader." When we take this idea and look at it from that perspective, we understand what being *subject to* our husband actually means.

For the military to succeed in war, its members follow proper rank and order. This enables the battle plan to work and our troops to be victorious. For example, a general can't win a war without the information he receives from the sergeant underneath him. The sergeant is closer to the battlefield than the general. He gathers what's happening on the frontlines. Then he takes that information back to the general for his consideration. This is where gathering, gleaning, and giving is fulfilled in the G³ War Strategy. The general then uses the sergeant's information to plan and make the decisions necessary to win the immediate battle and eventually the war. This is where our husband's A⁵ War Strategy is enacted. Once we gather, glean, and give information to the general in our ranks, he follows the simple plan explained below. The A⁵ strategy allows him to fully embrace his role as the general. As a husband and wife walk out their roles as the general and sergeant, they depend completely on the Commander in Chief for clear directions in the decisions they make. Just like with the military, God can see the entire picture of the battlefield from the air. Ultimately our victory relies on God's leadership as we march forward into war. Let's review the A⁵ War Strategy.

THE A5 WAR STRATEGY

Ask questions about the intel the sergeant has provided from the battlefront in your home.

Assess her opinion on the information, knowing a woman's intuition is critical to gaining insight into the enemy's plans.

Analyze the intelligence received, objectively consider the facts, and think through the options for a successful solution.

Approach the Commander in Chief in prayer and Bible study for the complete answer, knowing He knows the future and sees the hearts of those involved.

Ascend to your position over your kingdom and lay out the strategy for victory, empowering the sergeant to help implement the plan and win the war!

Now let's consider that a sergeant is solely dependent on the general's position. He cannot go to the battlefield and win without the general's leadership and decision-making skills. Since the general is farther removed from the frontlines, he's less emotional about his strategies and can base them on the bigger picture. He has a different perspective and can look at each battle with the end goal in mind. Once the battle plan is determined, the sergeant can take it to the frontlines and carry it out to completion with his troops. It takes both their perspectives to win, and they need each other to survive. Together, they combine their strengths and weaknesses and overcome their enemies and win the war for the nation. This is the same model God designed for husbands and wives.

WHAT'S THE WAR REALLY ABOUT?

The destructive cultural war around us is raging against our marriage and home. We're fighting for our relationships to survive, and as parents, we're fighting for the souls of our children and the security of their future. When we apply what we've learned from the example above, we realize we have greater strength when we depend on each other and work together as husband and wife versus waging war against one another. Without working as a team in the role and rank God has given us, the three-stranded model is broken. Thus, we can lose the war and end up as a casualty of divorce.

It's not uncommon for women to be able to focus on a task and work diligently toward a goal. The problem is the casualties we leave behind if we're barking orders instead of marching in proper rank. We can destroy or tear down our household by forgetting how and why we were created. We all have God given strengths and abilities that make us who we are as women. They are the same qualities that captivated our husband's heart and caused them to fall in love. Nevertheless, our skills must be used in the proper rank and order, or they become the same qualities that can cause a husband to run astray and go AWOL. The term *AWOL* is an acronym that stands for "absence without leave" meaning "a soldier has abandoned his duty with no intent to return." It's considered an act of treason.

Sometimes the cost is not as big as treason or divorce, but even in the small things there's still a price to pay. A few years ago, during a basement remodel, I made a decision that carried a large price tag. Dan had negotiated the price of commercial carpet tiles for the floors. He sent me to pick them up while he prepped the space. We lived fifty miles away, and when I got there, I realized all the boxes weren't going to fit into the van. With my *where there's a will there is a way* mentality, I resolved to somehow get them all home to finish the job as soon as possible. While standing in the parking lot, I made the decision to unpack all the tiles from the boxes and load them directly into the van. I should have called Dan to find out what he thought was best before making this determination. He had information I needed, but I marched ahead anyway. I didn't know he had an agreement with the seller to return any boxes left-over for a refund as long as the tiles were in their original package.

When we began to lay the carpet, it wasn't first quality. None of the seams matched. It wasn't even the same color as our sample. We got a great price on the carpet, but they sold it as first quality when instead it was seconds. Unfortunately, in my determination to bring all the tiles home without boxes, none of it could be returned. Luckily, due to our creativity, we laid it in a checkerboard pattern, so the matchless seams weren't an issue. However, it was still not the quality we thought we had purchased, and the tiles left over could not be returned for a refund. In my strong will and impatience, my decision didn't cost us our marriage, but it did cost us valuable time and money.

HOW DOES BIBLICAL RANK AND ORDER WORK?

According to Scripture, as our husband walks in proper rank, he's fulfilling his role like God the Father. It also means he's representing the role of Christ in laying down his life. Our ability to walk in our role as the Holy Spirit is fulfilled when we march as the sergeant. As defined in the previous chapter, we have a sensitivity that men don't possess called intuition. It's the most important weapon we can use on the frontlines. We see, feel, and sense what the battle really is on a day-to-day basis in our home. If you haven't tapped into this God given gift, you can start developing it now.

What do we do with the information we're intuitively gathering from the situations we see and sense around us? We use the G^3 War Strategy to gather, glean, and give. When we apply the military term *hupotasso* from Scripture, our job is to take information from the front-lines back to our husband the general, so he can use the A^5 War Strategy to design a battle plan to lead us to victory.

HOW DO I TRUST MY GENERAL TO LEAD?

If following rank and order is hard for you, examine your past. If the problem is a trust issue based on past disappointment or previous bad decisions, you can overcome your struggle. With the methods I'm about to share, an issue of trust can be overcome. Many times, mistrust originates from our relationship with our dad or a male parent figure growing up. If there was no male leadership in your life, then you may be struggling because you never learned to follow. Our trust in our husband must always go back to our trust in God the Father instead of our earthly father figure. God loves us, and we can trust him every time no matter how we grew up.

In my life, the father who raised me was a great provider, but he struggled with abusive tendencies. He was also unfaithful to my mom, so I had issues with trust. After Dan and I married, I still struggled. It wasn't until the day of my DNA test; I realized my relationship with my dad was not relevant to my ability to trust my Heavenly Father or my husband. The ability to trust our husband must only come from our Heavenly Father's perspective. Maybe you had a great dad or male role model as a child, and this isn't an issue for you. If not, you may struggle with trust as I did. You may have to go back to your point of reference and re-program your thinking to address how you feel. Scripture teaches we are to put away old thinking and reprogram or renew our minds. Ephesians 4:23 states,

And be renewed in the spirit of your minds; (KJV)

I accomplished this task by making a visit to the past. First, I made a list of my dad's good and admirable qualities. Then I thanked God for what was on the list. Next, I wrote a letter to my dad thanking him for those traits and what he taught me through them. Writing the letter is healing even if you can't deliver it. A letter to a deceased father can accomplish the same goal. Then I took an honest look at my dad's negative qualities and compared them to the characteristics of my Heavenly Father. My dad's negative attributes had been hurtful. At times, they created unhealthy or negative thoughts about men in general. Again, I had to get on my knees and ask the Lord to help me forgive my dad for the things he'd done that wounded me. Choosing to grant forgiveness is not for the other person. It's for ourselves. I chose to give my dad the same grace God's given me for the mistakes I've made. I asked God's forgiveness for holding on to hurt feelings toward my dad and for placing my feelings about my dad's issues onto my husband. I asked God to cover those mistakes symbolically with his blood he shed on the cross. I chose to forgive my dad and release him from punishment. Then I rejected the enemy and the lies I had believed commanding him to stop speaking lies into my life causing me not to trust my husband.

The clear understanding between my dad's qualities and Gods made the biggest impact. God had been honest, fair, trustworthy, gentle, loving, generous, kind, long-suffering, merciful, and faithful in his relationship to me. As I considered the things he had done for me, I realized God always responded differently than my dad would have responded. This helped me to accept my dad, realizing he had done the best he could. Despite his failures, I knew my dad loved me, so I chose to forgive, and you can too. Our Heavenly Father's love for us is far greater than any human's love, and he can be trusted completely. Matthew 7:11 teaches,

> *As bad as you are, you still know how to give good gifts to your children. But your heavenly Father is even more ready to give good things to people who ask. (CEV)*

If the trust issue is not related to your father figure but rather a past relationship like a former boyfriend or someone you've lived with, etc. that must also be addressed. If you have experienced a deep emotional or physical connection with a person other than your spouse that wasn't trustworthy, it can affect your ability to trust your husband's leadership. Even if the relationship ended and you weren't wounded, it can still be an issue. When we form an emotional or sexual bond with someone other than our spouse, we not only become connected to them in the physical sense, but a connection in the spirit is also formed. Have you ever run into an old flame, and despite being in love with your husband, seeing them made your heart race or took your breath away? That's an indication you've formed what's called a soul tie. A *soul tie* is "a connecting of the mind or emotions; ties to past relationships, hurts and wounds that cause your emotions or responses to be under the control of the connection to that person." That bond has to be severed for you to move forward in following your spouse. See Appendix A where I give directions on how to break that tie. This process will set you free and move you forward in the right direction. I encourage you to break that tie now because it is creating a strand of four in what God created to be a strand of three.

When we put our trust in our Heavenly Father and his design for marriage, we can find our security in him and trust our husband to lead. Our husband's actions may not always line up with God's character. After all, they are human, but so are we. So, how do we follow? First, we must establish a clear understanding of our role, as we learn from this book. Second, we must commit to fulfilling that role because we can trust God with our design. Third, every day we must pray for our husband to surrender to God's control. Fourth, we must believe as we walk out our role it will enable our husband to eventually find his way to walk out his. Last, we can trust that God has a plan for our lives, and we have assurance in that plan, as stated in Jeremiah 29:11,

"For I know the plans I have for you," says the Lord. "They are plans for good and not for disaster, to give you a future and a hope." (NLT)

God loves us more than we comprehend and because of that love we can embrace God's authority and plan. We can willingly choose to follow Jesus example and place ourselves in line with rank and order. If your husband's choices don't always make sense, remember God doesn't always make sense in the decisions he makes for our lives either. God always knows best because he sees the bigger picture. We must extend that same attitude of belief towards our husband as he sees the circumstances from a different perspective. He makes determinations based on facts and strategy instead of emotion. As long as we're walking in rank and order, we can trust our general has our rear guard and will seek to make the best decision he deems necessary.

WHAT IF THE GENERAL MAKES A MISTAKE?

Sometimes in war, a general makes a mistake and it might cost him a small battle, but that doesn't mean you'll lose the war. Just like any general, our husband can learn from his mistakes and use what he's learned to be victorious next time. If we want our husband to rise to the occasion and become the valiant leader we desire, we have to offer him the same grace and forgiveness God offers us when we mess up. When we show grace and allow them to learn from their mistakes, they'll be more likely next time to ask for more input and support before making major decisions. They'll be less likely to make the same mistake twice because they don't want to disappoint a loving, encouraging queen!

CROWNING POINTS

- Man and woman were created equal but not the same
- There is no victory without rank and order
- Rank does not make us less important, it gives us the win
- Trust your husband's lead as your Heavenly Father's plan

We've been designed not only for our husband's benefit but for our own. Falling into place in our rank gives us the freedom to embrace our strengths and conquer the enemy from the throne in our home. We hold the incredible power of salvation in our hands. Embracing our rank doesn't make us less important to the victory. It actually gives us the win!

Follow me as we learn what it means to embrace one of the most important things God commanded us to do as wives. That's where we're headed next.

Chapter 8

WILL YOU RESPECT THE KING?

At the core of our ability to follow rank and order is one of the most notable mandates mentioned in Scripture. Just as our husband has been commanded to lay down his life for the queen, God commands us to respect the king. This is not about respecting the person but the position. It doesn't matter whether we like him on any given day. It doesn't matter if he's not acting very noble. It doesn't even matter if we think he's a lousy leader, God commands us to respect his position regardless of his leadership style. If there is no respect in the kingdom, rank and order fall apart and the kingdom crumbles and crashes to the ground. Our Father gave us Ephesians 5:22 as our guideline.

Wives be subject to your own husbands, as to the Lord. (NASB)

In the original Greek, the words *subject to* are translated "respect". *Respect* is defined as "a feeling of deep admiration for someone or something elicited by their abilities, qualities, or achievements." God desires for us to willingly, without hesitation, show the general our respect. As we respectfully place ourselves underneath the authority of our Commander in Chief making him Lord over our lives, he calls us to also willingly place ourselves in a position of respect toward our husband to empower him to become the leader we long for.

WHY DID GOD ORDER US TO RESPECT OUR HUSBAND?

Of all the things God could have commanded us to do as wives, he chose this as a top priority. Why? Because he wanted to reverse what happened in the garden, through us actively choosing to do the opposite of what Eve did. Our Father in Heaven commanded men and women to each do the thing that comes hardest for us to do. Eve failed to show Adam respect in the garden by not seeking his advice or protection from the Serpent in her posies. Adam failed to love his wife unto death by crushing the head of the serpent that had come to steal his kingdom's peace. That's why it's in the very nature of our DNA to blow it on these two points. As a result, women struggle to show their husband respect and men struggle to love and protect their wives.

Sadly, many women choose rebellion toward this mandate by ridiculing their husband's wisdom and protection. Men on the other hand are often disengaged in their wife's world and become passive and disassociated from communication with the one they love. This is a dangerous precedent that can literally destroy our future and cause us to lose the palace life the way Adam and Eve lost their garden.

Our best step towards change is to embrace our responsibility and paint the picture to our children and the world that God has called us to paint. We respect them as Scripture commands, and they love us even unto death and this process creates the circle of love and the strand of three that can't be broken. It's all about love and respect. To gain a more personal view of this concept, let's consider the story of Abigail, a noble and powerful woman from the Old Testament who saved her entire household with one single act of respectful regard.

WHO WAS ABIGAIL?

Abigail was a mighty warrior and a woman of wisdom who captivated King David's heart with her grace and poise. As we already know, David himself was a valiant warrior and worshiper who slew Goliath as a young boy and became the King of Israel as an adult. In this chapter, we're going to explore the woman who transfixed him by taking a totally different approach to his heart. She related to him as a King long before he ever received the crown.

Abigail lived in the land of Carmel with her husband Nabal. She was known for her beauty and intelligence.[1] Her husband Nabal on the other hand lived up to the meaning of his name, "fool". In historical accounts, he's described as "mean and churlish". As we'll discover, he lived up to that reputation. According to 1 Samuel 25 where the story begins, the saga unfolds as Nabal and David's paths intersect. Nabal was very wealthy with a sizable estate and owned lots of servants and livestock. At the time, David and his men were hiding out in the hills near Nabal's property running for their lives from King Saul. When Nabal's herdsmen came out to watch their sheep, despite David's dire circumstances of hunger and need, he and his men never stole from Nabal's flocks. In fact, they provided protection when it was needed without receiving any payment. As the struggle to survive got more desperate, David decided to send some of his men to Nabal and appeal for favor and food. They made an urgent plea for generosity during harvest when food was plentiful. Nabal responded foolishly to David's request. He answered David's men with a trite, "Who is this King David, who is the son of Jesse?" In other words, "Who do you think you are that I should regard you?" He even suggested David was just a common thief.

In his disrespect, Nabal made David incredibly angry. As a result, David began to act like a fool himself with a plan to retaliate. He gathered four hundred men with their swords and set off towards Nabal's household to destroy him and everything he owned. One of Nabal's servants overheard the news of what David and his men had planned and quickly went to Abigail for help. When she heard the warrior was on a warpath headed her way, she got busy. She gathered a hundred loaves of bread, two hundred fig cakes, and loaded up corn, raisins, and sheep. She prepared them all, put them on her donkey, and took off to intercept the man of war. When she approached him, the Bible states Abigail got off her donkey, fell before David, bowing herself to the ground. She appealed to his kingly nature even though he had no crown. As a result of Abigail's appeal of respect, David changed his course of action. Abigail was a mere stranger showing David the honor due a king. She reminded him of what he was going to become instead of rebuking him for how he was behaving. She saw his potential and treated him as if he were already there. Are you getting the picture here?

As influential wives, we can choose to follow Abigail's example. That choice can motivate our husband to become the kind of ruler we desire to follow. Your husband may not be the leader you long for yet, but you have the power to help him ascend to noble character worthy of a king's post. I'm not recommending manipulation but exhortation and illumination. To *exhort* means "to encourage." To *illuminate* means to "light up or shine the light upon." If we believe in the destiny of our husband, we can move him in the right direction, shedding light on who God's called him to be, by showing him the respect Scripture admonishes us to give. In our role as the *Holy Spirit*, we can blow in and change everything by being who God has created us to be.

> *If we believe in the destiny of our husband, we can move him in the right direction, shedding light on who God's called him to be, by showing him the respect Scripture admonishes us to give.*

As a woman, we are beautiful and delicate like a breeze, yet powerful and strong like a mighty rushing wind. However, with the wrong attitude we can become like a storm tearing things apart. For many years I whirled around like a tornado, longing to be a quiet and gentle spirit yet not able to find my way to that place. Situations just never seemed to work out the way I imagined. Instead, I'd find myself frustrated and end up expressing my emotions like a typhoon, drenching everyone with words and responses that seemed out of control. This can become a vicious cycle for a woman. The more we try to walk in our role and fail, the more *storm like* we become. I knew my design, and I desired to walk in respect. Instead, I often found myself completely misunderstood. Then I had a life changing revelation a few years ago. I knew I was designed to be the *Holy Spirit*, but we can't be an imitator of something we don't actually understand. The role of the Holy Spirit in our personal lives gives us the model we follow as respectful wives. We can't empower the king of our home to stand on the battlefield of life and conquer the world if we don't walk in the wonder of the Holy Spirit while understanding the balance between the gentle breeze and the mighty rushing wind.

How did I learn the identities of the Holy Spirit?

As I began to explore all the characteristics of the Holy Spirit taught in Scripture, it brought reassurance and freedom to me in so many ways as a woman. I hope it does the same for you. This revelation came in the middle of the night while on a three-week family vacation visiting our son in Australia. As you can imagine, the trip was amazing. However, for five vastly different people of varying ages traveling around a foreign country for twenty-one days in an automobile, it can be a carload of chaos. Once the chaos and disrespect ensued, I began to pray for God to show up in the midst. It just so happened that the world renowned Hillsong Conference was going on at the time. Our son was a student there and managed to get us tickets for the last day. As we entered the arena, we learned that our pastor at the time from Gainesville, GA would be the keynote speaker, and we were surprised. As he began to speak, it was a topic he had preached just a couple of weeks earlier in the states. I sat there disappointed to hear the same sermon, until it suddenly hit me. If we had to fly halfway around the world to hear this message again then there must be something in it that we missed the first time.

When Pastor Jentezen Franklin began speaking, he spoke on the "Seventh Hand". His message explained how the number of *man* is six because we were created on the sixth day of creation. Man can only do so much with his own hands but when we add the seventh hand, God's hand, we become limitless in what we can accomplish. The number *seven* in Scripture represents *God* meaning "spiritual perfection". After the sermon that night, I began to pray and ask God why he wanted us to hear the same sermon twice. He began to show me clearly that as a wife and mother I'd been using my own hands to create a healthy home that only he could build. As a woman of power and strength we have to do our part, but our strength can only take us so far. We need the seventh hand, the hand of our Father, to reach in and do the rest. Dan and I had already recognized the roles of husband and wife in the triune image of Father, Son, and Holy Spirit. What I had never understood was how my role as the *Holy Spirit* was connected to my mandate of respect. God used this sermon to clarify his command. In Proverbs 14:1 it teaches us,

The wise woman builds her house, but with her own hands the foolish one tears hers down.

As women of faith, we have a choice to either build up our house or tear it down with our own hands through the respect we show in our role as the *Holy Spirit*. I realized that night I'd been working so hard with my own hands to build the perfect home I'd actually been doing more harm than good. I was overcome with brokenness for all the things I'd done that had torn down what God was trying to build. I asked for forgiveness for it all and instantly my right hand that had been injured for years was completely healed. I realize this might challenge your thinking if you don't know how you feel about healing, but God does refer to himself as *Jehovah Rapha*, "the God who heals us." You may recall seeing it as one of the names on the adoption papers in Chapter 3.

Over twenty-five years ago, when I was pregnant with our first child, I was diagnosed with having *carpal tunnel* in my thumb. I had lived with the pain for many years, and it had affected my ability to do certain things. On this night, after grasping everything God was saying about letting go of my family and letting him be God, I cried out for forgiveness in complete brokenness. Immediately my thumb pain was gone, and it has never returned. As I've shared before, I grew up in a chaotic, war-torn castle where disrespect was commonplace. As a result, I wanted my home to be perfect. From the time I was pregnant with our first son, I had wanted to control everything to make sure nothing destroyed the palace I was building. Little did I know my control was destroying the very thing I wanted to build. I was creating the chaos by disrespecting the freedom of others, including my husband. Once the truth came flooding in, I asked my family's forgiveness, and it changed the entire atmosphere of our Australian trip. It was as if they all sighed a sigh of relief.

Next, I did research on every single role of the Holy Spirit as taught in Scripture. That is what I want to teach you now. I believe this understanding will set you completely free of the things about yourself you might not understand and empower you to walk in noble respect toward the man of your dreams. This could change everything for you!

WHAT ARE THE CHARACTERISTICS OF THE HOLY SPIRIT THAT EMPOWER US AS A WIFE?

Regenerator - The Holy Spirit re-generates by breathing new life into the dead. As wives, we believe when no one else does. We breathe life into those we love who may feel hopeless. Wives flow through their homes as re-generators, giving confidence to the insecure. We proclaim, "you can do this," or "I know you can." We empower everyone in our palace through our faith, deeds, prayers, and resurrecting words.

Teacher and Guide - From the beginning of time, the Holy Spirit has been hailed as the one sent to lovingly lead into truth, causing growth and maturity to prosper. This is the very nature of a wife and mother as stated above in Proverbs 31. We can build. We guide into wisdom by teaching and preparing those we love for their future. We encourage growth and maturity while speaking even difficult truths as we go.

Reuniter - The Holy Spirit creates partnerships to bind hearts together in difficult times. As the heartbeat of the home, we sense when something's wrong in the relationships around us. We work to help bring hearts back together by seeking, speaking, and lovingly helping resolve conflict and reuniting relationships.

Intercessor - The Holy Spirit acts as God's presence within us and moves us to intercessory prayer for our family. As prayer warriors for our home, we are called to pray without ceasing and intercede in faith, giving birth to the answers we're waiting on. The Holy Spirit reaffirms us of God's love by interceding on our behalf. We interject God's love and truth into the situations in our home, reaffirming our husband and children that God the Father loves and cares for their every need.

Comforter - Following his resurrection, as Jesus ascended to Heaven, he told his disciples he would send them a comforter to sustain them with supernatural strength and hope. As a wife of noble character, we can sustain those we love by doing the same thing. We comfort our children, wipe away their tears, clean their boo boos, and bandage their wounds. Like the Holy Spirit, we hold them on our laps when someone mistreats or persecutes them reaffirming their identity as a child of a mighty King. As a wife, we encourage our husband when he doesn't get the promotion. We capture his heart with our comfort. We remind him he is our *hero*.

Silent Warrior - The Holy Spirit gives us grace to endure hardship and fight unseen battles when someone we love is accused or misunderstood. As women of respect, we encourage our husband to hang on, and press on. "You can make that deadline at work," or "you will get that raise." As mothers, we sometimes do battle in the here and now. We're the mamma who waits at the bus stop to have a discussion with the local bully. Nobody can stop a noble queen on a royal war path.

Empowerer - The Holy Spirit gives courage when we doubt and strength when we can't carry on. A woman will stand amid disbelief, hopelessness, and fear, and remind her family God loves them, and they can overcome. "You can give that speech." "You can win that race." "You can beat the odds." "You can get your miracle" because we intimately know the miracle worker. We lift the chins of those who are sad, mixing gentle correction with encouragement. We speak the truth in love like a warmhearted whisper.

Refiner - The Holy Spirit has always been the one to gently nudge us when we're hiding secret sin or walking in bondage. As intuitive women, we know when something's off in our home. Just like the Holy Spirit, we come alongside those we love and gently nudge them to tell the truth, to come forward and confess, and to pursue freedom. We work to create conversation, so the truth can be exposed. We long for healing and wholeness in our palace because it's in the heart of who we are. We don't like to sweep things under the rug. We want the issues in our home tidied up and the messes put away.

When we understand who we are and who God created us to be, we become the fragrance of hope in our homes, and we walk in full respect of our own identity and the identity of our husband.

HOW DID DAVID AND ABIGAIL'S LOVE STORY END?

After all the years of living with a fool, Abigail knew how to approach a king and David blessed her for coming. He thanked her for stopping him from shedding blood to avenge himself. He graciously received her gifts and sent her on her way, vowing never to destroy her household. She used her women's intuition, appealed to his kingly nature, and delivered her kingdom with respect. Upon returning to her castle, and I do mean castle of chaos, she found Nabal drunk. He was having a party and living up to his name. Despite his actions, Abigail was a woman determined to turn her castle into a palace. She recognized timing was everything, so she waited until morning to tell him what she had done, revealing then how close they had come to losing their lives. Waiting for the right moment to address a problem makes the difference in whether the problem goes or grows, and we can learn from her example.

The next day, Abigail exposed the details of her actions. Interestingly enough, Nabal went into heart failure and died ten days later. Abigail's life changed from that day forward. Soon after her husband's death, word spread to David that she was a widow. Upon receiving the information, he immediately decided to make her the queen by his side. He sent his servants to ask for her hand in marriage. I believe David wanted this fair maiden at his side when he took the throne because she knew how to appeal to his noble nature. Scripture doesn't tell us what he was thinking or feeling at the time, but I'm convinced he saw something in her that captured his heart on the road between his cave and her castle, and he wanted to carry her into his future palace. Her ability to show the respect due a king had changed his actions and won his favor. By bringing out the best in him, she became his heart's desire. We have the same capability when we speak to the leader in our husband by respecting his position.

How do you live out the role as the Holy Spirit?

As a woman who represents the Holy Spirit in your marriage, you can move everything in the right direction just by being the best version of yourself you can be. That's what Abigail did. She had other choices she could have made, but she chose to take the high road. That path led her out of trouble and paved her way to the palace. All she did was her best at the things she knew how to do. Every woman has different strengths and weaknesses. You may not know how to bake bread, but you can make your husband his favorite sandwich for lunch. You may not know how to make fig cakes, but you can pick up a half dozen cupcakes in his favorite flavor while you are out. You may not know how to load up a sheep and make a delivery, but you can make sure his wool pants are taken to the dry cleaners to save him a trip. You may not know how to ride a donkey, but you can drive him to the airport as an added blessing now and then. These may seem like trivial things, but they are acts of respect and consideration that can move your husband's heart in a new direction.

Just like Abigail, you may find yourself in a situation where your husband wants to head toward destruction like David, but you have the power to head him off at the pass. Abigail didn't beg and plead for David's mercy, instead she showed him who he could be by honoring him for his potential. She simply chose to ignore how he was acting at the moment. She didn't nag or scold him, instead she made a respectful appeal.

We can bring living water to the situation or a can of gasoline to the fire.

I know from experience when a knight in shining armor is acting like the court jester, we tend to react versus respond. That's not unusual. Remember, we have an innate desire to overthrow our husband's position like Eve. Because of how I grew up, the first thing I want to do when something starts spinning out of control is rise up like a tornado and tear down the situation to protect my home. That's never the best choice. When our husband is acting out of character, we have the same two choices as Abigail. We can bring living water to the situation or a can of gasoline to the fire.

I'm blessed and grateful because my husband has never been a *Nabal* kind of guy. That doesn't mean in three decades of love and marriage he's never acted out of character. Nobody is perfect which is why we needed a Father to adopt us out of our personal mess. Our husband isn't always going to be brave or show nobility when things get hard. All men have the potential to turn into *Adam* and let the serpent into the garden or overreact like a *Nabal* and become the serpent. When that happens, if we choose the path of Abigail and do something out of the ordinary, we not only fulfill our responsibility as noble queen, but we help restore the peace with respect. No matter what kind of chaos is headed our way, like Abigail we can choose to live as the quiet yet powerful *Holy Spirit* until the king in our husband arrives.

CROWNING POINTS

- ♛ Men are commanded to love even unto death
- ♛ Women are commanded to willingly respect
- ♛ Together love and respect create a circle of lifelong love
- ♛ Walking in our role as *Holy Spirit* establishes our respect
- ♛ Respect can turn a fool into a King

As we move forward, we'll explore our role as it relates to honor. Respect and honor are very similar, but their motivation is not the same. Follow me to Chapter 9.

Chapter 9

WILL YOU GIVE HONOR TO THE KING?

Honoring the man by our side is another important part of our role as queen because it helps bring stability to the kingdom. Although honor and respect are similar, they are not the same. Honor and respect go hand in hand and speak love to a king's heart, but they are vastly different in their motivation. Respect is having regard for a person's position. Honor is something given to someone as a gift motivated by love. It's about loving someone enough to honor them unconditionally even when they fail to command their post properly.

The word *honor* means "to give merit to a person, to show high respect and to esteem both in success and failure." In this chapter we'll explore the specifics of practical things you can do to give honor to the man by your side.

IS HONOR A CHOICE?

If you recall, respect was a command given to wives regarding their husband's position. Honor is a choice. God's been working on this part of my life from the day we said "I do". My desire to pay honor to the king by my side is really important to me. I believe this is a battle every woman must win for the covenant of marriage. We must maintain an ongoing attitude of honor for our husband's heart because *palace order* is at stake. As I've pondered my failures, I've come to understand honor is something I can choose to give even if the king of the palace is not acting honorable. In the military, respect is expected regardless of the actions of your superior, otherwise the battle plan fails. Honor is something we can either choose to give or withhold in the moment. We may not feel like honoring in the stress of life, but we can choose to honor anyway.

If you're disappointed in your husband as a leader and protector or not feeling attracted to him physically, I challenge you to look at yourself first. It may not be the reason for his failure every time, but it might prove to be the cause of his lack of courage. Men respond to honor faster than anything else we offer them other than sex. When they feel honored, they begin to love sacrificially. In the process, you might find yourself captivated again by his love and intimacy will naturally follow.

Despite our heritage from Eve, we don't have to act like her due to our new royal bloodline in Christ. I've learned whenever things get out of balance at our house, I must step back and ask myself, "Am I giving my husband honor?" regardless of whether I feel he's earned it or not. Sometimes when I can't be objective, I give him the freedom to give me his opinion. If your marriage is in trouble, look at the *honor* factor to see if it could be the answer to the *why*. If you're in a situation where you can't ask your husband's opinion, ask a female friend who'll be honest and has witnessed your relationship. Marriages have been saved by asking for forgiveness for attitudes of dishonor and then pouring honor back into the foundation of the palace.

WILL YOU CHANGE HIM OR EMBRACE HIM?

We may see the potential in our husband for nobler deeds, but that doesn't give us the right to seek to change him. Many women marry in hopes of remaking their husbands into what they want them to be instead of embracing them for who they are. Scripture tells us that we are the clay and God is the potter. He molds and shapes our lives with his gentle hands into whom he desires for us to be. Remember, God is the only *maker*. I've come to realize after wasting years trying to help Dan become what I wanted him to be, a wife doesn't have that kind of power. We weren't commanded to *change* our husband. We were commanded to love him with honor regardless of his flaws.

When Dan and I were married, I was determined to change his eating habits. I had a degree in health education, and I wanted him to eat healthy because of its long-term benefits. Even though my motive was pure, my desire to change him was not in God's plan. We had many arguments the first few years of marriage over food. I'd grown up on a farm with vegetables as the main course, and he grew up in the city where vegetables were his least favorite thing to consume. He thought green salad was lime Jell-O with marshmallows, nuts, and cream cheese. The most frustrating issue was that his opinions about food weren't based on their taste. Most of them he had never tasted. Talk about a firestorm of conflict. I tried everything, including disguising vegetables and hiding them in other things. It created distrust and every time we sat down to a meal, he automatically asked, "What's in this?" I wasn't doing him any favors and I certainly wasn't stabilizing our kingdom. He felt hurt and dishonored because I did not love him just the way he was.

When our children came along and were old enough to have an opinion on food, they started following his example. If *daddy* didn't like it, they didn't eat it. Our differences became more pronounced because of the added influence he had over them. I was at my wits' end when I realized something needed to change.

WILL YOU TRY SOMETHING DIFFERENT?

After years of conflict over this issue, I determined to try something new. After all, the definition of *insanity* is "doing the same thing over and over while expecting something different in return." Clearly the definition of *sanity* must be "doing something different and expecting something different in return." I quit talking about food and just focused on my own eating habits. After all, my diet was not the best it could be either. I did more reading and research on several kinds of healthy eating methods. I found one I believed would benefit my health long-term and made me feel great. I started eating healthier with consistency. Out of surrender to my lack of influence and my desperate need for change in this area, I also resorted to prayer. I prayed for Dan to realize the importance of his health. I prayed he would recognize how important his example was to our children, and I prayed for his taste in food to change. Amazingly, my prayers began to be answered. He began to experiment with food and try other things that I cooked when I stopped trying to control what he ate. I was amazed as I watched

God perform a literal miracle. I learned a lot from that experience. I realized that when a woman pushes, a man will almost always pull in the opposite direction. I learned that loving our knight despite the kinks in his armor goes farther than trying to bang the kinks out with a hammer. I soon recognized that prayer goes farther than a power struggle.

> *Loving our knight despite the kinks in his armor goes farther than trying to bang the kinks out with a hammer.*

We weren't created to rearrange the man in our lives; we were created to honor them and allow God to change their character. Our Creator knows how to create and mold a life much better than we do. The Bible proclaims in Isaiah 64:8,

> *Yet you, O Lord, you are our Father. We are the clay, and you are the potter. We all are formed by your hand."* (NLT)

WILL YOU SPEAK WITH AN IGNOBLE TONGUE?

Unlike Eve, when the house shakes from the cultural quakes around us, the kingdom will not tremble and fall if we're living in nobility giving honor to our king. Whatever we speak to we get. If we speak to a serpent, we'll get a serpent, so to speak. When we speak with an ignoble tongue, we end up with a king that won't lead or one who can't because he's crippled by the fear of disappointing the queen. We can end up with a king who sits on his throne and does nothing if we disregard his leadership or question his wisdom every time he seeks to lead as the general. Using our tongue to dishonor the general will cause leadership to collapse.

Let me share another part of our story. Seems every time we've taken a road trip outside our kingdom, the chaos comes. Apparently, directions and driving can be an issue for many couples. In fact, it's often featured in comedy sketches. I'm known as the *back-road queen* at our house. If there's a better path to a location, I'm going to find it. In my country girl mind, it's better to travel the way the crow flies because it's shorter and more direct. The problem with shortcuts is they aren't Dan's idea of fun. He prefers taking the most logical route with main roads and freeways. To him, it's faster according to his mathematical calculations. For me, driving a new way every time is about adventure, which flies in the face of logic. Logic is a great leadership quality for a general. It's a trait that helps a king make great decisions when it counts in battleground experiences. However, it can also get in their way of fun or spontaneity.

This difference in our thinking created an ongoing problem for Dan and me. The first few years of marriage, every time we got in the car to go somewhere, we ended up in an argument. He wanted to logically travel while I wanted to give my opinion and travel over the mountains and through the woods. Out of love for me, he might follow my advice, but if it turned out I was wrong, he would get angry and act like Adam in the garden of guilt. He would blame me for choosing the wrong path. If he didn't follow my advice and chose to go the logical way, I proceeded to complain all the way to our destination. Have you ever been there?

Here's the solution to the problem I recommend. "Let them lead, ladies!" Your husband is an adult. He knows how to drive. He has a plan, and he would like the freedom to follow it. That's what generals do. We should just enjoy the journey. Look for interesting things along the way to distract you from your frustrations. I often use it to catch up on social media or read through a large pile of junk mail. Sometimes I make a note of new places I want to visit next time we travel that way.

Honor is letting our husband lead even when we think we know a better way. Relax and let them be who they are now, so they can become who they were created to be tomorrow. You can take the back roads when you're the one driving.

WHAT ABOUT TONE OF VOICE?

I'm going to be completely honest here. This is my greatest struggle because it's not too far from being a mighty rushing wind to a testy tornado. Even when our message is important, tone of voice can discredit the message. If we speak to the king of our home with contempt, they will almost always feel dishonored and unloved. Since we are naturally more emotional, tone of voice is something that constantly has to be monitored. As a cheerleader in high school growing up in a household that was quite loud, it's been a battle. I can sometimes find myself raising my voice just in regular conversation. I've always had a strong and boisterous voice.

I didn't realize it was a problem until we had children. Children are great mirrors and reflect what they see. When I would speak to them about poor behavior, they would often ask me to stop yelling. I would step back and think, "I'm not yelling, I'm just speaking firmly," but to them, my tone and body language was speaking volumes. I soon realized I'd been doing this to Dan our entire married life and didn't even know it. It was a habit that had to be broken.

Have you ever spoken harshly but your emotions had nothing to do with what you were saying? As the heartbeat of the home, we can easily express our feelings out loud for everyone to see even when it's not about them. Sometimes circumstances can encourage harsh tones. Yelling at the baseball field is not a problem, but if you want a palace and not a castle, the volume has to be toned down at the royal residence. In our present home there are very few walls, so it can get quite loud. I've had to try to identify the issues creating chaos and then put a plan in place to curb the problem. One example creating dishonor at our house happened every time I would call my family to the table to eat. I would find myself yelling at the top of my lungs in a hateful tone to get everyone's attention, especially if I had to call them more than once. My solution was to implement the old-fashioned dinner bell. I hung a bell on the kitchen wall, and when a meal was ready, I rung it. This alleviated the yelling, and everyone was much happier when they arrived to eat. The Scripture encourages us to pursue a quiet and gentle spirit. It starts with prayer and assessing our tone. The best thing to do is observe yourself and take notes to discover where tone issues occur the most. You can come up with a solution for each one. Over time the problem can be alleviated.

WILL YOU ALLOW INTERRUPTIONS AT THE PALACE?

Another problem that creates dishonor is interrupting conversation. If we constantly interrupt others when they speak or express their feelings, we're cutting off the flow of healthy communication. Anytime we shut down conversation, even with our children, we're showing dishonor and damaging relationships. Listening well is an act of honor.

Women can have strong opinions, and we often rush to express them. I've had to work hard at waiting until it's my turn to speak or it's the appropriate time to express my thoughts. As logical thinkers, men like to think before they speak. This can be an issue for women because we often think and speak quickly and expect the same in return.

By realizing how men communicate, we can relax and enjoy the silence. All we have to do is gather and give information and then walk away. Accept the pregnant pause at the palace. It will allow the king to process the information and come to us when he's ready to talk. We'll gain a greater understanding on communication differences and how to overcome them in the next chapter.

Interruptions can also be an issue within a family especially during serious family conversations or weekly meetings. To curb this problem, we have implemented a palace plan. As we hold our family meetings on Sunday afternoons each week to discuss our schedules over the next seven days, we write the details on a large calendar that hangs on the kitchen wall. During the meeting, we don't allow interruptions. To keep order and to make sure everyone isn't talking at once, we grab a small item to pass to the person who has the floor when it's their turn to speak. If someone else has something to say they must raise their hand and then the item is passed to them. You can use any funny object for this purpose. It can be as simple as a serving spoon or even a stuffed animal, or you can pick up something fun at the *Dollar Tree* and give this idea a shot.

WILL YOU RALLY THE TROOPS?

Rallying the troops, in the midst of a battle, is key to winning the war. As queen of the palace and sergeant of the battlefield, we must rally our children around our cause to hold the kingdom together. Some things we've struggled with in our children are the result of false beliefs. In today's culture, most family television shows portray the husband and father as the laughingstock of the family. Often the dad in the storyline is the one trying to keep order in the home, yet no one seems to care or want to hear what he has to say. He comes across weak and out of touch, and sometimes even goofy. This isn't the example of leadership our children can afford to look at on a regular basis. It's like propaganda used in WWII when they dropped false messages from the war planes over the skies of Leningrad. The enemy wants to taint the palace perspective of the general, causing everyone to see him as weak and unable to lead. Those false beliefs can turn hearts in the wrong direction.

Rallying the troops, in the midst of a battle, is key to winning the war.

As a mother, it's our mandate to make sure our children don't harbor false beliefs toward the general in our homes. Years ago, I began to notice that one of our children was struggling with a condescending, disrespectful attitude towards authority. After I gathered and gave that intel to Dan, he followed up using the A^5 War Strategy. He realized it was directly tied to a specific channel on television being watched during free time. It was notorious for comical shows undermining parents. When he understood the root of the problem and how our child's opinions on authority were being formed from that influence, we removed the source and the subscription to the channel was cancelled. The hearts of our children must be full of honor. Having a tarnished view of our role as their leader over the kingdom can lead to heart break down the road. Never fail to address dishonor in the camp. It's our responsibility to be watchful and proactive in guarding ourselves and the hearts of our children. We can lead them to follow the king in our home by our example as we show honor.

CROWNING POINTS

- Honor is a gift we choose to give out of love
- Honor speaks love to the heart of a man
- God can change our husband as we accept them fully
- Rallying the troops is key to keeping the kingdom safe

A breakdown in communication is a top cause for divorce. In the next chapter we'll learn how to effectively communicate with less castle chatter. Healthy communication is the sparkle that can turn your castle into a *Cinderella* palace.

Chapter 10

WILL YOU SPEAK TO THE KING OR THE FOOL?

This chapter is all about communication. Having a peaceful palace is based on healthy principles of conversation. If communication is unhealthy, there is nothing to stand on when chaos comes. You can't survive without communication in rank and order. You can't communicate respect. You can't communicate honor, and you can't resolve conflict without conversation. How many times have you looked around a restaurant and witnessed complete communication shutdown at the tables surrounding you? Culture has replaced conversation with emotionless electronic chatter. I recently told Dan that if something didn't change, before you know it, we'll be seeing couples texting their vows to each other while standing at the altar saying, "I do".

Let's explore communication on a much deeper level by examining the differences between women and men in this area first. There's been a great deal of research on the subject of communication differences between the sexes. One study found men tend to talk slower than women. The late Dr. Gary Smalley, a family counselor, founder of the Smalley Relationship Center, and author of forty books on marriage taught that men on average say only 125 words per minute while women say 250 words per minute. As a result, women typically use 25,000 words per day while men only expel 12,000. This means what women say really matters because we have twice as much opportunity to create chaos with castle chatter.

A few years ago, I was impacted by a quote I heard in a women's Bible study. I have no idea where the saying originated, but whoever coined the phrase was brilliant.

Inside every man there is a king and a fool. If you speak to the fool, he will act like a fool, but if you speak to the king, he will act like a king.

As I processed this thought, I realized how true it was. It was evident in the story of Abigail and King David. It's evident in our communication today. Scripture even supports this idea in Proverbs 15:1,

A gentle answer turns away wrath, but a harsh word stirs up anger.

We can probably all think of a time in our marriage when either we or our spouse acted out of character and looked foolish. When communication is strained, everybody can start acting like a court jester. Proverbs 26:4-5 warns,

Don't answer the foolish arguments of fools, or you will become as foolish as they are... (NLT)

There've been plenty of times in disagreements with Dan that winning the argument was more important to me than the damage being done through the conversation. I've found myself unmoved by compassion over a point of view. It's in our nature to think we're always right, but if we want the king in our husband to step up to the throne, we sometimes have to lay down our desire to win the battle. Losing an argument can be more productive than proving our opinion over doing what's best for the kingdom. Choosing to speak to the king versus the fool is one of the most important aspects to keeping communication healthy and strong. It's also one of the easiest parts of conversation that we often disregard. Especially in today's electronic, cell phone driven world where social media offers us an opportunity to communicate without being fully engaged. If someone starts to speak to us like we're a fool online, we simply unfriend them or block them from our life. The reality is, we don't have that option in marriage. According to the verse from Proverbs foolishness breeds more foolishness in conversation. That's why arguments escalate. Scripture is true, a gentle response somehow seems to dissipate the issue. We can either fuel the fire of foolishness or diffuse the frustration in the kingdom. Answering foolishness with wisdom helps reveal the truth in the situation, giving us the power to bring out honorable conversation.

> *We can either fuel the fire of foolishness or diffuse the frustration in the kingdom to bring out honorable conversation.*

WHO WERE KING DAVID AND HIS WIFE, MICHAL?

As I began to search for more evidence in Scripture to help us apply this lesson to our marriage, my steps led me once again to the Old Testament. There, I considered the biblical account of King David and Michal, another of David's wives. Unlike Abigail whose story ended in palace peace, Michal's saga landed her living in complete isolation. She chose to speak to David the King like he was a fool, and he fulfilled her expectations.

As a result of his victory over Goliath, King Saul promised David his daughter's hand in marriage. David chose Saul's daughter Michal. She had fallen in love with him while he played music for her father at the castle. Sadly, Saul grew to despise David over time out of envy. David had developed quite a reputation as a great warrior and Saul became jealous. It had something to do with young David killing Goliath as the King hid in his royal tent. From that point forward, the people in Saul's kingdom celebrated David's success, and the king boiled with hatred.

King Saul's envy was exhibited in the most hurtful way. As David played his harp and sung in service to the king, his music brought him great comfort. Saul was tormented by his own sin, and over time his jealousy became so great he sought to kill David. Finally, it got so chaotic at the castle, David had to flee for his life out the window of the castle as Michal, his young bride, stayed behind at her father's estate. As a result of his leaving and Saul's hatred, Michal was handed off to another man in marriage by her father, while David ran for his life.

After many years of hiding, circumstances turned as King Saul and his men were defeated by the Philistines. As a result of disobedience to the Lord, Saul lost his crown and died tragically on the battlefield. King David valiantly stepped up to the throne, moving back into the palace where Michal rejoined him as queen. King David ruled nobly, and the Lord favored him giving him continued victory over his enemies. The one thing that disturbed his empire was the missing *Ark of the Covenant*. The great king longed for its return as it represented the history and deliverance of God's people out of Egypt. It contained the glory of God and the king wanted it restored to its designated position in the capital city. David and his men finally accomplished this goal bringing it back home to Jerusalem.

When the great procession of its return began to enter the city, David was so excited for its arrival he tore his clothes and danced before the Lord in worship. The Scripture implies he was without his normal armor or royal attire. Instead, he wore an *ephod*, "a type of undergarment worn under a king's clothing". King David and his kingdom were in full celebration with dancing in the streets which wasn't unusual after such a significant event. Unfortunately, as his wife Michal watched from the palace window, she was enraged. Upon David's return, she scolded him for his behavior and belittled his accomplishment. II Samuel 6:16 describes,

> *As the ark of the Lord was entering the city of David, Michal daughter of Saul watched from a window. And when she saw King David leaping and dancing before the Lord, she despised him in her heart.... She came out to meet him and said, "How the king of Israel has distinguished himself today, going around half-naked in full view of the slave girls of his servants as any vulgar fellow would!"*

Michal's response was sharp and detrimental to their marriage and the palace became a castle of war in an instant. We aren't told why she got angry, but most likely she was prideful and considered his dancing an embarrassment to the throne and beneath her status as queen. Whatever the case, David scolded her for ridiculing his worship and then banished her from his bedroom for good. Michal never birthed an heir to the throne in a time when being barren was considered a curse. Her actions had tarnished David's great accomplishment, and he wanted nothing to do with her as a result. Let's recap the story. Michal labeled David's behavior as foolish and spoke harshly to the king as if he were a fool. David had been acting like a victorious king, but as a result of her rebuke he foolishly chose to walk away and turn his back on his bride.

WHY IS COMMUNICATION IMPORTANT TO INTIMACY?

Communication is just as important to intimacy in a marriage as any other part of the relationship. Intimacy is how we were created to become one flesh, but it starts with conversation. Tone has been a struggle for me, but several years ago, as God began to change my tone in conversation, I began to see changes in my husband and his leadership. I was working harder to speak to the king versus the fool and it soon produced a difference in our marriage. Dan began to share how he felt he had not been the leader God wanted him to be. He even told me there had been times he allowed me to take the lead in areas of our marriage where he knew he was AWOL. He determined not to allow it anymore.

I could have taken offense to his comments, but instead, I felt loved and shocked at his bravery. I realized I was about to give up some authority I'd taken in areas of our lives that weren't mine to command. At the same time, I understood my need to feel protected and safe was finally going to be met. I began to feel a stronger attraction for Dan physically because he had finally stepped into his position as my knight in shining armor. That was something I didn't expect, but his bravery was very attractive. Finally, I had met a man who would put me in my place. If you are struggling with physical attraction, consider your tone. It could be the issue. If so, adjust your communication skills and watch what can happen to your sex life.

HOW DO WE DEAL WITH DIFFERENCES IN CONVERSATION?

As I mentioned at the start of the chapter, men and women are vastly different. Women have twice as many words in a day that they need to use than men. How do we deal with this difference? First, we realize that even though we may feel the need to talk, our husband can feel like he's drinking from a fire hose if we don't use wisdom in timing. Take the opportunity to assess your situation before pouring a bucket of conversation over his head the minute he arrives home at the end of the day.

Another key to communication success is not waiting to the end of the evening to share all your thoughts and emotions. Otherwise, it could be a late night. By taking the time to open up and share earlier in the evening, you can alleviate the lack of sleep later, and more importantly allow for time to bond physically.

One effective way we've found to stay connected is to set aside fifteen minutes of focused conversation and catch up from the day's activities when we first meet back at home. Once our children arrived on the scene, we called this *mom and dad time*. We gave them a few simple rules. They were not allowed to interrupt our conversation. If necessary, we used a kitchen timer with an alarm that would let them know when our time was up. This is a great way to teach children how to honor marriage. Nothing grows peace in the heart of a child more than seeing a mom and dad protect their relationship and show one another love through words. There have been times when our children were young and seemed to be having trouble with obedience. It never failed it was a busy season when Dan and I had been missing our *mom and dad time*. The minute we implemented it again, their behavior would change for the good. Communication between a husband and wife are a direct link to well-behaved children.

DO WE SAY WHAT WE MEAN AND MEAN WHAT WE SAY?

In case you haven't noticed, men and women can say exactly the same thing and mean something totally different. When a man says, "I don't have anything to wear," what he really means is, "I don't have anything clean." When a woman says, "I don't have anything to wear," what we really mean is, "I need to go shopping!" When our husband lets us know "We need to leave by six"? If we are not careful, we'll interpret that as, "I need to be ready around six, but no later than six-fifteen." Men are typically more prompt than women when it comes to being on time. If Dan says we need to leave by six, he means we need to leave by six on the dot, or we'll be late.

This misinterpretation can lead to chaos. For example, getting ready to go somewhere used to be a source of contention early in our marriage. I don't like being late and neither does he, but it takes a lot longer for a woman to get ready because of all the steps required, if you know what I mean. We finally found a solution that seems to work well. First, we placed a clock on my bathroom counter set for ten minutes earlier than it actually is. Then I asked Dan to announce to the entire house fifteen minutes before time to walk out the door. Then he gives another gentle reminder around five minutes before departure. Finally, he lets us know when there's one-minute remaining. He's always ready before me, so sometimes I even call on him to give me a hand by getting my jewelry or my shoes. Once we put this plan in place and everyone was on board, it worked. Now, we're rarely late.

DO YOU SPEAK WOMANESE?

Think back to your childhood. Do you recall playing with dolls and creating conversation or talking to yourself? I remember those *Barbie* days. Ken says, "Hello, Barbie, would you like to go on a long walk on the beach so that we can talk?" Barbie replies, "Oh Ken, how did you know that is exactly what I have been longing for?" Girls, that was our preparation for conversation as an adult. Boys, however, are a completely different breed. Their play tends to involve noises and one-syllable words. As they hold a gun, they shout, "Bang, Bang!" When they push a car they say, "Vroom, vroom!" This doesn't prepare them very well for lifelong interaction with the opposite sex. Have you ever been in a conversation when you start talking and your husband responds with a grunt or a "Hmmm"? It's reminiscent of an engine humming like the matchbox cars they used to roll across the floor. Although guttural exclamations like the Marines' "Oorah!" are common in the military, grunting is not proper etiquette for palace living. As a woman, we desire more than "Yeah", "Uh huh", or "OK". We have to encourage our husband to get past shallow interactions into the depths of real conversation if we want to feel loved in the way we desire.

Understanding our spouse's intent and not just their words can also be especially important. For example, men tend to think when a wife says, "I want you to be more affectionate" that we're interested in sex and that might be the last thing on our mind. For a woman, affection can be touching, snuggling, or hugging and not necessarily sexual in nature. It might take a while to help your spouse understand this difference but being open and honest is the best policy. If you aren't interested in sex, just let him know in a loving way exactly what you need and be very specific otherwise it could ruin the entire evening and crush his sexual ego. If a man wants to snuggle, more than likely he wants to have sex. Out of love for him, sometimes our joy is in meeting his need to protect him from what the world has to offer.

One of the practical ways we've improved sexual conversation is with a night-light in our room. If one of us is interested in a bed chamber rendezvous, we turn it on at any time during the day. If the other spouse is not interested or isn't feeling well, they have the freedom to gently turn the light off. The key is staying sensitive to the other person's needs. No one should turn the light off more than twice in a row for the health of the marriage.

If conversation begins to shut down, the enemy can infiltrate the kingdom and attack. When we tune into the communication differences between us and the king and queen converse, the kingdom is well protected, and the enemy has no way in. It's like raising the draw bridge and removing the entry points to keep us out of the enemy's grasp. Healthy correspondence provides a force field of protection around our entire domain.

WHAT ARE THE FOUR LEVELS OF COMMUNICATION?

In war and life, communication happens at different levels. In the military, they use briefings to provide details on enemy tactics to create plans based on current facts. A general will often ask for a deeper analysis from his leading sergeants to get their gut feeling on what the information means. That's where we come in as the sergeant on the frontlines in rank and order. Just like in the military, our kingdom communication needs to convey intelligence and marching orders at all four levels of communication.

❖ *Intellectual* – conveying detailed information
❖ *Emotional* – sharing feelings about a situation
❖ *Physical* – body language expressions
❖ *Spiritual* – God's guidance and direction

Let's consider each of these levels in depth, so we can understand them.

Intellectual

Most men are comfortable with "*just the facts.*" This is typically the level of discussions they use at their jobs and the method they tend to operate in most of the time. Logic and intellect dominate this type of conversation. It's their natural language, but not so much for women. We want emotional conversation. We need to feel connected to our spouse through conversation. Below are a couple of things Dan and I have implemented when having intellectual conversations to try to overcome this difference.

a.   *Repeat what you think you heard*: Because men and women think differently, what you say is probably not what each of you hear and vice versa. As we mentioned earlier, we can both say the same thing and mean something totally different. The best way to fix this issue is to repeat back to each other what you think you heard them say. This can resolve problems before they start. Many arguments start over misunderstandings. Repeating what you hear puts you ahead of the curve and also has another benefit. It makes you a better listener. Remember, you don't have to use the same words when you repeat back what you think you've heard. Proactive listening prevents chaos.

b.   *Always verify*: Many times, misunderstandings can have severe consequences. Several years ago, on a Friday evening before our weekly family night, Dan decided to give our dog a trim. Afterwards, our daughter was going to give him a bath. She started the bathwater and yelled at me, "Watch the tub, please," as she descended the stairs to the basement. Rachel didn't verify that I had heard her. About fifteen minutes later,

I heard the bathwater running and realized what was happening. As I ran into the bathroom, I went flying across the floor and landed face up in three inches of water. No one could hear me yelling for help from the basement. After I pulled myself together, I ran down the stairs just in time to see water pouring through the ceiling from the bathroom above. Instead of spending the evening playing games, we spent the night cleaning up the water-logged basement. Miscommunication can have dire consequences if we don't verify what we say or what we think we've heard.

Emotional

Let's face it ladies, emotional communication isn't usually hard for us. We typically don't have issues with showing emotion as the heartbeat of the home. On the other hand, one of the hardest areas for men to conquer is the *feelings* side of communication. Not only is it hard for them to share their feelings, it's sometimes hard for them to handle ours. Our emotional input is essential in the chain of command. Men need our emotional side, but how we communicate emotionally is crucial. If we're not careful, we can shut down their feelings by stepping on their conversation when they try to share. We want to understand what our general's thinking and feeling, but they often pull back if we jump too soon to give them our opinion. Remember, we gather and give information and lay it at their feet. Then they ask questions about what we think and how we feel about it. If we wait until they ask, giving them time to share, we'll gain the insight we need, and they won't shut down.

> *Our emotional input is essential in the chain of command.*

Emotional communication can also be conveyed through voice inflection, tone, and body language. Over 80% percent of what we say is understood by what people see. We can mask what we say with our words, but we can't mask how we feel with our body language. Men tend to be less easily read, and even though men have trouble expressing their feelings, when they do, it's real.

One of the biggest challenges we face is how to share our concerns without using over the top emotions that cause us not to be heard. The real struggle for men is the balance between sharing feelings while not coming across as weak instead of strong. In a crisis, a woman is looking for strength in leadership. Be sensitive to the fact that this is a juggling act for men and requires an extreme amount of grace on our part as a lady in waiting. Our husband will get there a lot faster if we're gracious and patient as he tries to share his thoughts and emotions. I've made the mistake of rushing in to counter or reiterate my point of view while Dan was trying to share. It's never paid off. When a man does share, he's looking for someone who'll listen. If it's not you, he can be tempted to find someone else to hear what he has to say. Patiently listening is another way to raise the drawbridge.

Physical

Albert Mehrabian, who did a famous psychological study on communication also researched body language and discovered it's an important part of expressing ourselves. It's so significant, it can even affect outcomes in political elections. During the 1991 presidential debates between George H. W. Bush, Ross Perot, and Bill Clinton, Bush looked down at his watch as the audience began to pose questions. This visual gave everyone the impression he didn't really care about the people. This played into his opponent's hands and cost him the presidency. Crossing our arms during conversation can also make us appear closed and uninterested in what's being said. Communication is not just talking, it's listening with our eyes, ears, and body. In our kingdom when someone speaks, everyone in the conversation should look the speaker in the eye and position themselves to engage in what's being spoken.

Growing up, I remember coming home from school wanting to talk about my day. My mom would often be reading the newspaper. I realize now that the mail must have arrived daily just before I did, but I can remember feeling ignored. As a result, when I want to talk to Dan or the children about something important, I need their undivided attention. If I don't get it, I find myself saying, "Are you listening?". As people of nobility, we have the right to be heard because our Commander in Chief declares that we are valuable, and he gives us direct orders every day. For that reason, both you and your husband should do whatever is necessary to show respect and honor as you convey feelings, emotions, and insight about whatever battle you're facing. In turn, the person listening should give their undivided attention. Today many of us struggle to keep our eyes off our phones when our husband or children speak. As a new royal decree, learning to listen is a must. Turning off your phone at dinner, weekly meetings, or important discussions could be the key to your marriage survival.

As a final note, since body language is so important, when discussing emotional topics, it can also include nonsexual physical touch such as hugs, holding hands, and cuddling to show love without saying a word. Gentle touches let your warrior know you love him, and he's the most important thing in the world to you. Of course, there's also the physical part of intimacy to convey romantic and erotic love. This part of nonverbal communication during foreplay and intercourse is also important for a healthy marriage. Physical touch is part of the marriage bond God said was "very good".

Spiritual

The deepest and most important level of communication is connecting spiritually. We can never truly become one until we're connected in mind, body, soul, AND spirit. It's the deepest level of communication with another human being, and it's essential to marriage. Our enemy knows how important it is to the unity in the kingdom, so he fights to prevent spiritual bonding from happening.

Our first spiritual level of communication begins with adoption by our Heavenly Father. If we don't have a vibrant, deep relationship with him, we'll have a hard time connecting spiritually with our spouse. The triangle diagram we covered earlier clearly paints this picture. The closer we move to our Heavenly Father in communication through our personal prayer time, Bible study, worship, and spiritual discussions, the closer we get to one another. As we grow and share what we're learning with the knight by our side, the deeper in intimacy with Christ and each other we'll grow. It's the beautiful three-faceted strand we've been discussing that's not easily broken.

WILL YOU BECOME COMPLETELY ONE WITH THE KING?

In this last section, we provide visuals to clarify the deepest level of communication. As mentioned, God uses strands of three throughout his Word. They represent strength. This is about the strand of three that forms the basis of the various levels of communication we've just discussed. As man and woman created in God's image, we have three distinct entities reiterated by Paul in I Thessalonians 5:23b,

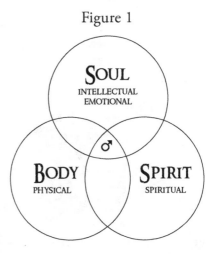

Figure 1

May your whole spirit, soul and body be kept blameless at the coming of our Lord Jesus Christ.

Mankind consists of body (physical), soul (intellectual and emotional) and spirit (spiritual). As shown in this Venn Diagram.

Figure 1 shows the way God created us in his image. The Soul is the place where our mind, will, and emotions make our decisions. They determine whether our Body (Scripture calls this flesh) or our Spirit (where the Holy Spirit dwells once we're adopted) will rule our lives by the decisions we make. As king and queen of our kingdom, we operate in all three areas.

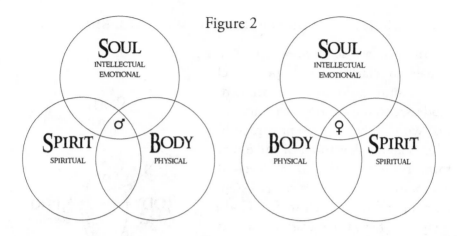

Figure 2

Figure 2 shows no connection between husband and wife. They are living separate lives in every way. This is what happens when communication completely breaks down, creating an extremely dangerous situation in a marriage.

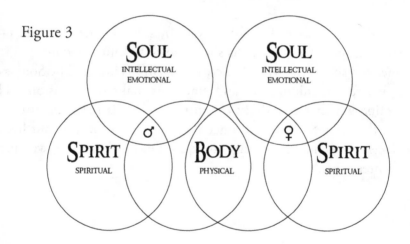

Figure 3

Figure 3 shows a single connection through physical intimacy. Even though this is an important part of marriage, if sex is the only way you communicate, it leads to an empty, superficial relationship usually based on lust. There's no security because there's no emotional or spiritual bond. That's why men can have the common one-night stand without remorse, but women walk away devastated by the lack of connection. It's easy to see there's very little overlap outside the bedroom, leaving the relationship feeling rocky, inconsistent, and insecure.

Figure 4 illustrates how a couple can grow deeper and begin to connect intellectually, physically, and emotionally. The bond grows stronger, and they grow closer, but the two are still not completely one flesh.

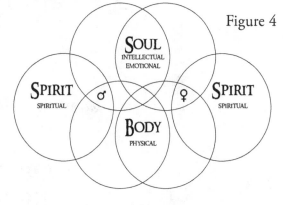

Figure 4

Finally, *Figure 5* shows complete unity where the two become one flesh. The couple is now connected on every level, i.e. mind, body, soul, and spirit. This is the secret to a fulfilling marriage. The king is fully united with his queen in one flesh. This is the goal of marriage. We completely step into our royal position as king and queen when we become one intellectually, emotionally, physically, and spiritually. This is the key to complete communication giving you and your spouse the win over the obstacles that may come your way. Complete unity is what empowers us to rule our kingdom well!

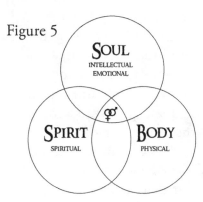

Figure 5

CROWNING POINTS

- 👑 You can bring out the king vs the fool with your words
- 👑 Women have twice as many words as men; use them wisely
- 👑 Always repeat back what you hear
- 👑 Communication at all four levels brings unity and success

If we want to unlock the secrets to communication in marriage, we must actively seek to connect. The more we become one, the more peace will prevail! Next, lets dive into living in nobility by confronting disorder so the kingdom can be restored.

Chapter 11

WILL YOU LIVE BY NOBILITY IN THE KINGDOM?

The topic we are digging into in this chapter is accountability. *Accountability* is defined as "an obligation or willingness to accept responsibility or to account for one's actions." This quality by definition seems to be greatly lacking in our world today. Nobody wants to be responsible for their choices while wanting the freedom to do as they please without the fallout of the consequences. It's no different today than it was in the Garden of Eden six thousand plus years ago. Once the first couple chose to disobey God, they each blamed another for their choice. If we want to rid our lives of chaos, we have to choose to live by *responsibility*. Integrity requires us to take responsibility for what we do as well as hold others accountable if their actions are affecting or harming our relationship. Without accountability nobility is absent.

Would you be willing to be dishonest on behalf of your husband? Would you willingly do something to protect his behavior even if it went against God's word? If we plan to live as the virtuous queen of our palace, we have to be willing to hold our husband accountable when he's leading us down the wrong path or heading us off of a cliff towards clear destruction.

HOW CAN WE RECOGNIZE ADAM AND EVE'S BEHAVIORS IN OUR KINGDOM?

As we've already discussed, Adam and Eve wandered from God's path and their lives quickly went astray. In this chapter, we're going to back up and clearly mark their behaviors, so we can spot them in our lives and confront them head on. Identifying wrong behaviors is half the battle to overcoming them, and it makes it easier for us to recognize the enemy's attacks before the battle begins. Don't get me wrong, Dan and I struggle sometimes with the *curse* of Adam and Eve because it's in our human DNA. Once we clearly defined their behavior, it gave us the advantage over the enemy. He uses the same tricks over and over, generation after generation because he's not very smart. He has nothing new in the weapons department. Satan used the same schemes with Adam and Eve that he uses on you and me today.

ADAM	EVE
Passive as protector	Disrespect towards leadership
Apathetic in taking action	Disloyal to her husband
Cowardice towards the serpent	Easily deceived and led astray
Self-absorbed vs. selfless	Pushy and persuasive
Follower vs. Leader	Leader vs. Follower
Blaming: "It was this woman"	Blaming: "It was the serpent"

Dan and I have agreed that we can't write a book on marriage if we can't be honest about our own relationship. We can look back over our past and remember specific instances where Dan exhibited the *Adam* qualities listed above in different circumstances that arose, and I have exhibited all of *Eve's* at some point or other. Do you recognize yourself in any of those behaviors? During our thirty plus years together, there have been times I've gotten greedy for power. I

We can either walk under the curse of Adam and Eve or walk under the covering of Christ as God's blessed, adopted children.

can relate to being pushy and blaming Dan or the enemy for choices I've made. With this understanding, we have a decision to make. We can either walk under the curse of Adam and Eve or walk under the covering of Christ as God's blessed, adopted children. The wrong choice will cause the kingdom to fall into the enemy's hands.

WHO WERE ABRAHAM AND SARAH?

Abraham and Sarah were another powerful pair with a destiny in God's plan. They were direct descendants of Adam and Eve. They, too, began to wander away from the promise God had made them, leading them to wrong choices, wrong plans, and a wrong future. As the story went, God told them to leave behind everything, and he would show them where he wanted them to go. He wanted to birth a nation through their obedience. On their journey, God made an appearance and gave them a promise they would have a son in their old age. As they continued their trek without clear direction or pointed destination, they landed at the gates of the city of Egypt. Prior to arriving, Abraham stepped out of his role as Sarah's protector because he was more worried about protecting himself. He became consumed with fear of what Pharaoh would do if he found out he was married to Sarah. He thought the King of Egypt might kill him and take Sarah as his bride. Apparently, she must have been a "hottie". As they approached the city, he asked her to lie to Pharaoh and tell him she was his sister. He thought if Pharaoh believed their story; he would spare his life. It seems they'd forgotten God's promise, or they didn't believe him. That's why they took circumstances into their own hands. Abraham wanted to lie to protect himself and the lie required Sarah's participation.

I know what a beautiful woman you are. When the Egyptians see you, they will say, "This is his wife." Then they will kill me but will let you live. Say you are my sister, so that I will be treated well for your sake and my life will be spared because of you. Genesis 12:11-13

Lying rarely pays off. As a result of their deception, Pharaoh took Sarah to be his wife, thinking her to be unmarried. Fortunately, according to Scripture, he never slept with her, jeopardizing God's plan for their future. As a result of their wrongdoing, all of Egypt became extremely ill bringing a curse on the entire nation. Pharaoh questioned them, and they admitted the truth. He practically ran them out of the empire, so he and his people could be restored to health. Sarah suffered by agreeing to lie for her husband instead of lovingly reminding him of the importance of telling the truth. Many times, if we avoid holding our husband accountable to the principles of noble living, the same behavior will continue. Twenty years later, Abraham asked Sara to do the same thing as they approached the city of Gerar. Once again, the king took her to be his wife. Again, God protected her, and they were run out of town.

Can you imagine your husband letting you marry two total strangers under the pretense of being his sister instead of his wife? Just think about how she must have felt not knowing what to do or what would happen. I'm sure she felt abandoned by the man meant to be her knight in shining armor. Each successive mistake where nobility is abandoned can lead us farther off the path that God has for our lives. Sadly, as God was about to bless Abraham and Sarah not just with one child but "descendants that numbered as great as the stars", they reached the point of desperation again. This time the results were far worse. They feared God's failure to keep his promise about giving them a son. As a result, Sarah encouraged Abraham to sleep with her maidservant Hagar, so she could birth them a son. They doubted what God had said just like Adam and Eve, and chaos began to run rampant. Their choice is still creating chaos in the Middle East today.

WILL YOU COVER UP THE TRUTH FOR YOUR KING?

Scripture is clear; we are to follow rank and order submitted to our husband's leadership as he is submitted unto the Commander in Chief. However, for rank and order to work properly, our husband must be dedicated to the principles of God's word. If our husband is doing something or asking us to do something that goes against principles of integrity, God's given us a means to protect ourselves. It's called *confrontation* which means to "face up to and deal with a problem or difficult situation."

As I thought about Sarah's vulnerability, I was reminded of a time when Dan failed to protect me and instead chose to protect himself. It's not nearly as serious as Abraham and Sarah's issue, but I did experience what I imagined were some of her emotions. Not long after we were married, I attended a business dinner with Dan. I was introduced to everyone at our table. A man, whom I would not consider a gentleman, made several sexual comments to me when Dan left and went to the restroom. I was shocked, to say the least. When Dan returned, I secretly told him what had happened. I'm sure he was shocked and didn't really know what to do. To be honest, I'm not sure what I expected him to do, but I wanted him to do something brave and noble like whip out a sword and dual to the death. Instead, he did nothing. In all fairness, things were different then than they are today. Dan wasn't sure if he or the other guy would lose their job. The mistake we both made was ignoring what had happened and not bringing closure to the situation. Over time, I came to realize that Dan's lack of response had caused me to doubt his love. Like *Adam*, by choosing not to protect me from a serpent, the serpent had created a lie inside my head. It caused me to take on an *Eve* identity and take charge whenever we were in a threatening situation because I didn't feel I could trust him to protect me. The lie also affected our intimacy. When a queen doesn't respect her king, she certainly doesn't want to follow him to the bed chamber. I finally realized that to be set free from its effects on our marriage, I had to revisit the situation with loving confrontation and forgiveness.

There are other circumstances that lead to the need for confrontation. One example is when a wife feels the need to lie to cover up for her husband's addiction. Women who are married to addicts of any kind often lie for their husbands to protect their reputation. Unfortunately, by doing so it allows the addiction to continue without forcing them to take responsibility. In today's culture, it could easily be an addiction to alcohol, drugs, or even pornography. Lying to cover up habitual behaviors is enabling the behavior to progress. Often this is a picture of an unhealthy, co-dependent relationship where the enabler is addicted to the behavior, so they can control the kingdom. If you're one of those couples, then seek outside help from a faith-based addiction counselor or pastor to break this cycle of *Adam and Eve* behaviors.

Another example of destructive cover-up is irresponsible adultery. A few years ago, I coached a young woman who lost her husband to adultery after several years of marriage. Unfortunately, it wasn't the first time he had an affair or acted inappropriate with another woman. Each time, he confessed it after it was over, and she forgave him. He often blamed the other woman for his mistake, just like Adam. Sadly, she never forced him to take full responsibility for his actions. They never sought help from a counselor or coach, and he never faced consequences for his behavior. She didn't realize the long-term threat to their marriage until he walked out the last time with another drama queen. He left under the curse of *Adam* blaming her for all their marital issues.

I would be skipping a particularly important problem today if I didn't share one of the most difficult situations wives are facing. I encountered its devastation in another coaching situation. In this case pornography was involved.[2] The wife was seeing red flags in the bed chamber. It was an embarrassing subject, so she tried to handle it alone until he finally walked out. There are times when a wife might be faced with a difficult, embarrassing situation she tries to ignore in hopes it goes away. That rarely happens. The first time we see serious warning signs where our health, home, or marriage are in trouble and the enemy has a cannon aimed at us, suit up in your armor and prepare to confront. If that doesn't work, get help.

WHY CHECK MY EMOTIONS BEFORE CONFRONTING THE KING?

Before we can confront a difficult circumstance, we first must check our emotions. As women, we are much more passionate about emotion. It's part of our design, but in our weakness, we can lose control and let our feelings lead. Many women have a difficult time hiding their emotions and can sometimes express them too freely. Take a look at Facebook, Instagram, or some other type of social media. The posts that seem to be dishing out a little too much information are usually by women.

There are typically three ways we express what we feel. There are those of us who express freely, those who process calmly, and those who repress in denial. We'll call those who share too much information, *expressors.* They dangerously share private details meant to stay in the kingdom versus the public square. There's another kind of expressor where what they share is just too loud and explosive. I believe every woman at some point, whether with her children or spouse, has experienced the guilt that goes with this expression. Sometimes things just get the best of us. The key is whether this is the exception and not the rule. If you don't struggle with this, it probably means you've got great coping skills and you process emotions more calmly like Abigail when she approached King David. This leads us to the next kind of expression.

This group we'll call the *processors*. Abigail falls into this category of women. Learning to process more calmly should be our goal and something we consistently strive for. If you are self-controlled in difficult times as Queen Abigail was, you're a woman of true noble character. Instead of panic, she created peace by turning her situation into a blessing of intervention. We can all learn from her example of what to do when trouble heads in our direction.

The third example of how females sometimes respond we'll call the *repressors*. I also refer to this style of relating as the *sweeper*. When trouble comes, they sweep the issues right under the rug and hope nobody trips. If you're a sweeper, you might want to consider cleaning out the dust and beating out the rugs, just don't do it all at once. Maybe you could consider uncovering the issues slowly unpacking one thing at a time. If you're living in denial about issues or hiding them in hopes that others will never notice, be careful because eventually someone will trip and fall over the rug and get hurt. This can be very traumatic to the family unit.

What if Abigail had been a sweeper? Her entire household would have crumbled underneath a pile of destruction. Her problem was too big to try to hide, so she calmly processed the reality and moved forward with a solution. Small issues may seem like something a sweeper can hide but eventually all the little things stack up to one big pile of problems. I've honestly done all three types of responses. Only one has paid off. I can tell you from experience with expressing and repressing, both required a lot of cleanup and rebuilding. As a repressor, if you don't think you can handle uncovering the hidden issues alone, you can seek out a relationship coach who can lead you through the process. *Processing* is the only way that leads to peace in the palace. Our focus on healthy processing in this chapter is all about *confrontation*.

WHEN CRISIS HEADS TOWARDS THE PALACE GATES, THEN WHAT?

Our first responsibility as a woman of intuition is to pray for wisdom. James 1:5 proclaims,

If any of you needs wisdom to know what you should do, you should ask God, and he will give it to you. God is generous to everyone and doesn't find fault with them. (GWT)

Next, we obey what the Lord tells us to do. He'll give us one of two answers, duck and watch or confront. My best friend says when God wants to deal with your husband, sometimes we have to move out of his way, so he has a straight shot for our husband's jaw. Our greatest weapon if God says to *duck and watch* is to pray while God deals with our husband's heart. Otherwise, we can be standing in the way spending all our time telling our king how wrong he is. Sometimes we can be speaking so loudly they can't hear the voice of God over our yelling, which only hardens their heart. It keeps God's Spirit from being able to move and bring conviction about their actions. In reality, sometimes we have to sit down, shut up, and pray.

If God tells us instead that we are to confront, we must prepare. A confrontation may be scary or sound complicated but it's really not that hard. It means we must talk to our spouse and share what they are doing that's contrary to what God expects.

IS IT NAGGING WHEN WE CONFRONT?

When we nag instead of lovingly confront it makes us victims in a broken system of poor communication.

Confronting our husband does not mean we take the issue and use it like a hammer to beat him over the head. If we take this approach, they'll often run the other way and never listen to what we have to say. The culture often calls confrontation by a wife *nagging*. The word *nag* means "to annoy or irritate with persistent fault-finding or continuous urging; to harass or badger." Early in our marriage, I sometimes found myself saying the same things over and over about an issue. I realize now, I was really trying to implement the tool of loving confrontation. I just didn't know how.

God has asked us to willingly walk under our husband's authority, and to protect us in that position of vulnerability, he also calls us to willingly confront in love when required. If we don't learn how to use this shield God has given us, we can end up not being protected from a serpent. When we nag instead of lovingly confront, it makes us victims in a broken system of poor communication. To use confrontation in the wrong way would be like trying to use a screwdriver to drive a nail into the wall. We must use the right tools to drive home a point in our husband's life if his actions don't line up with God's design. We confront in love to restore him to a right relationship with the Father.

CAN YOU GIVE ME AN EXAMPLE ON HOW TO CONFRONT?

Now let's look at the narrative of a noble Queen named Esther in one of her bravest moments. She found herself in a life and death situation requiring her immediate intervention with her king. Xerxes was the King of Persia. His first wife fell from the throne after "a full 180 days" of partying at the palace when she refused to honor him before his guests. We'll learn more about their story later. As a result, Xerxes chose Esther to take the queen's place and this fair maiden turned her king's castle into a palace before he knew what hit him. She was highly favored by the king.

King Xerxes knew nothing of Esther's blood line or nationality. She was a Jew by birth, and an orphan adopted and raised by her Uncle Mordecai's family. Once the decision by Xerxes was made that she would become his queen, her heritage seemed unimportant. However, a short time later her lineage became the key to her future. At this point, things began to get a little out of control. As the chaos mounted, Esther found herself holding the future of an entire nation in her hands. As I pondered that thought, I realized, as the chaos mounts in our home, we can rise above the chaos if we are willing to live by the truth and confront when confrontation is required and literally save the kingdom.

Unfortunately for Esther, there was an enemy in the camp who had a lot more power than she did. He was plotting for revenge. His name was Haman, and he had been given the highest seat of honor among the nobles in the King's court. We'll skip the details, but his family history was intertwined with the Jews and his hatred for them went back many generations.

When King Xerxes awarded Haman his high-ranking position, he found himself embarrassed by the fact Mordecai, Esther's uncle, would not bow a knee as Haman passed him at the king's gate. Mordecai refused to show him respect because he only bowed his knee to God. This action embittered Haman, and he determined to find a way to have all the Jews, including women and children, killed out of selfish rage. One day while consulting King Xerxes, he saw an opportunity. Esther 3:8 states Haman misled the king with false information and convinced him it was not in the best interest of the throne for him to tolerate the existence of the Jews in his kingdom any longer. This information led Xerxes to make a decree that all the Jews would be annihilated.

Unknowingly, King Xerxes didn't realize this included his Jewish bride, the beautiful Queen Esther. Mordecai sent word to her about the decree as the entire Jewish race was at stake. Her life and crown were on the line, as well as the well-being of her husband and his kingdom. She could let her people perish, or she could put her life at risk by approaching the throne. She chose bravery over cowardice for the sake of their salvation and determined to confront him in the presence of Haman. Sometimes our confrontation will be about saving our personal kingdom, at others about saving our Heavenly Father's reputation.

First, Esther prepared herself by fasting and praying. Fasting is one of the three commands we're given in Scripture as children of the King. If you've never done it before, Pastor Jentezen Franklin has several resources that can help.[3] Fasting is a tool we can use to rid ourselves of all distractions and focus completely on hearing the voice of God for direction. Esther knew she needed a clear answer on what to do because approaching the throne without invitation was a crime punishable by death. Before we confront our king, we can pray for wisdom and clarity to make sure we're supposed to move forward. In doing so, we may realize we're supposed to duck out of God's way and let him do what only he can do, or we move forward to confront.

WHAT'S YOUR MOTIVE?

We can't expect to approach our husband and succeed if our heart is in the wrong place. Our motive must be pure and unmotivated by selfishness. We must only confront because God has asked us to. We must understand our primary goal is to restore our husband to a right relationship with God and not to ourselves. Our husband may never apologize to us. Our motive is to help him reconcile his relationship with Christ. If this relationship is restored, then the relationship to us will also eventually be restored. We may never hear the words we want to hear like "I'm so sorry" or "Please forgive me." Those words are the words meant for the Heavenly Father first. Once that happens, God can soften your husband's heart and move him to say to you whatever needs to be said.

WILL YOU GO WITH COURAGE?

Next, Esther, who was determined to do the right thing, had to grab hold of courage and devise her plan. Confronting our husband will require courage especially if the subject is a sensitive one. Esther approached the King humbly and he received her. We cannot approach our husband with a prideful, righteous arrogance. Instead, if we follow Esther's example and approach with meekness, he'll be more likely to listen.

With no expectations, Esther gathered her courage and approached the king, presenting him with an invitation. It's always best to presume nothing and extend an invitation to our king, trusting he'll accept our request for conversation. Esther extended an invitation to the king to join her for dinner. Once she served up a banquet fit for a king, he promised her anything she requested. Instead of stating her intentions, she chose to invite him to return for a second dinner party. On the second occasion, she spoke the truth regarding the plot against the Jews. Maybe she wanted to make doubly sure he'd be willing to hear what she had to say, or maybe she sensed he wasn't prepared. Whatever the case, her patience and persistence are qualities we need when we approach the love of our life in confrontation.

DOES TIMING REALLY MATTER?

We must carefully plan when and how we'll confront our king. Just as Esther realized, we must also admit that timing is everything. You know your husband best. If he is unusually irritable after a long day at work, then approaching him at the end of the day would be poor timing. It's not clear in Scripture when Esther approached the king. A few years ago, a movie came out called *One Night with the King.* Aside from the creative liberties taken in the movie, it was historically based on the Bible account of Esther and Xerxes. In their theatrical narrative, she approached the king before he left for war. For us, that can be translated into approaching our husband before a stressful time at work. Maybe confronting over a cup of coffee in the morning or a nice romantic dinner over the weekend would have better results.

We can learn from Esther's model by not confronting at the first dinner and waiting until the second. I have to believe that her female intuition and God's leading revealed it wasn't time. We have the Holy Spirit who can guide us. We must be patient. If you start to speak to your husband and sense it's not going to go in the right direction, change your course of action.

When Dan and I first got married, if I had something to say, I felt like I would explode if I didn't say it right away. If I sensed he didn't want to hear what I had to say, I determined to say it anyway. My mentality was, "The truth must be told!" Once I proclaimed the truth, I always felt like a bull in a china shop, something was left shattered, crushed, or broken. I had either broken my husband's heart, crushed his spirit, or shattered his male ego. Our relationship required a lot more glue when I was finished.

If you start to confront your husband and sense the timing is off, Esther's best advice would be to wait and pray for wisdom and try again with a new batch of courage. We must be patient and not anxious on timing in confrontation. Most importantly, pray for God to prepare your husband's heart to receive what you have to say. God prepared King Xerxes heart by depriving him of an entire night's sleep between the first and second dinner.

WILL YOU SPEAK THE TRUTH IN LOVE?

Speaking the truth in love is one of the most important aspects of confronting your king. I remember an old saying I believe my mom used to say, "You can get more flies with honey than vinegar." If we put ourselves in our husband's shoes, I think we can realize the truth is hard to hear. It means coming face to face with our personal failures. The truth is easier to swallow if it's spoken with loving lips. In the days of royal courts, one had to be summoned before approaching the throne. Esther knew the risks and bravely went anyway. When it came time for her to speak the truth, she spoke clearly with respect to his authority while explaining her circumstances. Remember, men interpret love as respect and honor. Esther respectfully accepted the fact King Xerxes still had the final say regarding Haman's plot to kill the Jews. Your husband's response is up to him. Before approaching, we have to prepare ourselves as Esther did to be willing to accept the king's response, no matter what it is. It doesn't mean it can't change over time.

CAN YOU PRESENT THE EVIDENCE CLEARLY?

There were times early on when I'd approach Dan to confront him, and he'd ask for specific examples as proof. It was almost like I was presenting my opening arguments to the court. Unfortunately, I was like the young legal assistant who had not prepared. I soon learned I had to have the evidence to back up my case or the conversation turned into arguing and went nowhere. Presenting evidence doesn't give us permission to bring up old crimes that have already been discussed and forgiven. We can't throw the past in our husband's face, or we'll lose our credibility. It does mean when presenting the proof, we provide a couple of recent examples to calmly make our point. It's okay to prepare ahead just as Esther did. You can even put notes on your phone of examples when they occur, so you won't have to remember them later when the time comes. You're not keeping score; you're just keeping good records. Esther clearly explained why she needed to address the crisis with her king. Then she gave the evidence that proved the guilt of the enemy.

WHAT DO YOU DO IF IT DOESN'T WORK?

Another step toward loving confrontation is being able to recognize when the issue can't be resolved. Sometimes it takes time for a knight in shining armor to accept the truth even if we have followed all the right steps provided by Esther's example. That's where the convicting power of the Holy Spirit comes in. Sometimes when a person has sin in their life, they're blinded by it and can't see what they're doing. Once we share the truth; it takes time for the Holy Spirit to complete its work.

You may find, as Esther did, that your king is willing to address the issue immediately. Esther's king declared a verdict and death penalty against Haman immediately. If your husband doesn't respond as quickly, then be encouraged by John 8:32,

The truth shall set you free.

Once the truth is spoken, God's spirit has the freedom to move. If, however, your husband absolutely refuses to hear what you have to say it may be time to seek counsel from an objective third party. Sometimes the truth is easier spoken by someone outside your relationship that your husband trusts. If your husband refuses to seek counsel, then prayer is your best resource as you seek how to best cope with the issue.

You may need to gather another warrior to help you pray. Esther's victory was won with a team. She requested Mordecai and all the Jews join her in prayer. He and the Jewish people fasted and prayed for three days on her behalf. You can enlist others to pray for you without divulging all the details of what is going on by simply asking them to pray.

I have a friend who has sought marriage coaching from me recently. Her husband is considering leaving her. She has shared the details with me but not with her friends or family. She has only let them know they need prayer. If you share too much information with friends and family, it can destroy your husband's reputation and bring him dishonor. It's important we protect their reputation with people in our inner circle so that when and if he has a change of heart, they won't be tempted to reject his new reform.

What if he isn't adopted?

The last thing I want to say about this matter concerns a husband who is not adopted by the Father. If he hasn't chosen to be adopted, you can't approach him in the same way as you would if he has. You can follow Esther's example in methodology, but you cannot use Scripture to back it up. 1 Corinthians 2:14 warns,

But people who aren't spiritual can't receive these truths from God's spirit. It all sounds foolish to them, and they can't understand it, for only those who are spiritual can understand what the Spirit means. (NLT)

In this case a queen would confront her king based on what is decent and noble. You will simply have to appeal to the king in him versus the fool without using the Bible as part of your reference material.

If we're going to live by nobility, we must be willing to live by the truth. We have to be honest with ourselves, honest with God, and honest with our spouse as a part of our role to hold them accountable. Just like Esther, you may be the only one who can confront the king and restore the kingdom to bring salvation to your household. With God's grace we can walk forward in courage and confront with honor if we approach the king in love.

CROWNING POINTS

- Identify yourself as an expressor, processor, or repressor
- Lovingly confront the king to restore him to the Father
- Check you motives first
- Fast and pray if required
- Speak the truth in love
- Let God do the rest

Speaking of nobility, let's move forward and learn how to avoid tarnishing our husband's crown.

Chapter 12

WILL YOU POLISH HIS ROYAL CROWN?

When it comes to being noble, we have to consider the crown. King Solomon, considered one of the wisest kings to have lived, definitely had strong opinions about the queen and the crown. Why wouldn't he? After all, the only thing that tarnished his crown was a woman. It wasn't one in particular. Instead, it was his own poor decision to marry too many women at the same time. He became the perfect test study on what not to do. In the midst of his chaotic choice, he seemed to realize which women he admired and which ones stood out as probably more work than it was worth.

In this chapter we'll focus on the later part of a verse we looked at earlier in "Will You Help the King?". We've talked about what it means to be our husband's crown and glory. Now let's discuss what might tarnish the royal crown if we shame the kingdom. Let's read Proverbs 12:4 again,

A wife of noble character is her husband's crown, but a wife who causes shame is like rottenness in his bones. (CSB)

I don't know about you, but I don't want to bring physical illness or rottenness to my husband's bones. I would rather be a crown of glory than decay. The weight of this Scripture paints a terrible but clear picture of just how important encouraging our husband to walk out his mandate as the king of our kingdom really is. When we abdicate our role as help meet, we tarnish their royal crown. If we refuse to acknowledge their nobility, we break their headdress. In days of old if a queen ridiculed the king in public, it was considered an act of treason. If she refused to support his efforts in leadership, it was considered shameful. You and I can either create bravery in our leader by encouraging our king in his role or create doubt in his mind about his ability to lead if we refuse to follow. Every king needs to believe their queen would follow them to the ends of the earth if necessary.

Just before Dan proposed, he asked me an important question, "Would I be willing to follow him wherever he needed to go?" He explained that he wasn't sure where the future would take him. He wanted to know if I was open to the idea. My answer was "yes." At the time I had no idea why this question mattered, but through the years, I've grown to understand the weight of the answer. Queens must not get weary on the journey.

WHAT HAPPENS WHEN WE REFUSE TO FOLLOW THE KING?

Following our king may not only be about following their lead around the kingdom but leaving one palace for another. It can be about moving to a new location. When I think of how often the wives of our military have to move, its heartbreaking, but it's part of their duty. It's required to fulfill their task as a soldier's wife. Having a woman that will follow them wherever the war takes them creates an atmosphere for their success as they step onto the battlefield. Our husband's may not fight literal wars, but they fight for our families every day on many battlefields, and our role as queen is to support them, so they can win the war.

I spent time encouraging a young woman a few years ago that had grown weary of the moves attached to her husband's career. They had moved eight times, but on the latest move she made it clear to him it would be her last. Her reasoning was all the sacrifices in moving she had previously made, earning her the right to stay put this time. I cautioned her it was risky to her role as a wife. After all, this was the job he had when they married, and it provided for their kingdom's needs. She went into the marriage with her eyes wide open knowing following him to the ends of the earth might be required. Sadly, months later, he chose a new queen and moved on to the next destination, and she's still sitting in the last state they landed in, alone.

WOMEN HAVE INTUITION BUT WHAT DO MEN HAVE?

As stated, our intuition helps us walk out our powerful role as sergeant to our general. Men also have a special quality we don't possess to help them walk out their lives as noble leaders. It's called the *male ego*. Many see the *ego* as a negative quality because it's often confused with arrogance. Sometimes these two words are even presented as synonyms, but they aren't. I think we can understand the differences and the importance of the ego by considering both their definitions. The word *arrogance* is defined as "conceit, pride, and egotism." However, *ego* is defined as "a person's sense of self-importance, self-respect, self-worth, and self-confidence." Proverbs16:18 clearly defines the problem with arrogance,

Pride goes before destruction, a haughty spirit before a fall. (ESV)

Pride can be detrimental to a kingdom. It leads to destruction making arrogance undesirable in a king. However, ego has importance to the kingdom's survival. This quality is the very thing meant to make a man a warrior, so they become the knight in shining armor we desperately want them to be. As you may recall, a wise woman can build her house, but a foolish one can tear it down with her own hands. The male ego is very fragile, and it must be built up. If we nurture the ego in our man, it will give them the courage to rise to the occasion and lead. If we tear it down, they'll become disengaged from the battle.

HOW DO WE BUILD THEIR EGO IN A HEALTHY WAY?

I'm sure you've heard war stories about soldiers throwing themselves onto a bomb to save an entire regimen. The reason men lay down their lives for the sake of others is due to respect within the platoon. If we want to help our husband stand up and fight for our family, we must build our warrior's ego, so he will save our kingdom. Bravery in the Scripture is noted many times usually during battles between God's good people and the evil of another kingdom. Many times, when *bravery* is mentioned, the word *warrior* is also listed. In Chronicles, a book in the Bible that records the lives of God's chosen people, fathers and their descendants are all listed in chronological order. What was so striking to me as I read this book was the description of the fathers with

details about their character and their leadership in war. For example, 1 Chronicles 5:24 records,

They were brave warriors, famous men, and heads of their families.

I Chronicles 7:40 records the descendants of Asher,

All of these men were men of Asher, leaders of ancestral households, choice valiant mighty warriors, and chiefs among princes. (ISV)

Why would God want to record not only the lineage of his people but also their character as a warrior? I believe he wanted to give notice to those men who followed the mandate of their design. They were notable because they were doing what they were created to do. They rose to the occasion and bravely led. As a help meet to your husband, you can stand up and support his call to duty by nurturing his male ego through encouragement. Your nobility can strengthen and encourage his nobility.

WHAT IS THE FLAG OF SURRENDER?

We are our king's royal tiara, and if we damage his image, we not only tarnish their crown but ourselves. The male ego can easily be wounded. If a wife speaks embarrassment or ridicules a husband, he interprets it as treason in his heart. It means his queen has gone over to the other side and surrendered to the enemy's ranks. There's an example in the Bible that quickly comes to mind, and we can learn from this queen's mistake. She was the first queen to King Xerxes, before Queen Esther joined him on the throne. He put Vashti away and married Esther because of Queen Vashti's betrayal. Vashti tarnished her husband's royal crown beyond repair. It was a time of war and the king had called all the dignitaries and rulers from other lands together for an important summit. War strategy and politics were being discussed over a month-long party. It was a summit to determine how to conquer their enemy.

In the meantime, Queen Vashti was having her own little tea party with all the dignitary's wives. I can imagine they were getting their hair and nails done while talking about the new fashion trends in royal robes. Unfortunately, she was having so much fun with all the girls she refused to answer when the king beckoned. He requested her presence to dance before their guests, which was customary at the time, yet she refused to go. As a result of his embarrassment, Xerxes banished her from the kingdom. She had tarnished her husband's image before the most important people in the land. It was a crucial time to his leadership during a season of war. She had undermined his authority, and he took her betrayal to heart. Xerxes was embarrassed, and he chose to end his marriage. He put her away for the act of betrayal. Historically, he had no choice because weakness at a time of war by his most trusted confidant could cost them the kingdom. Some historians believe he had her beheaded although this is not mentioned in Scripture.

Let me give you a modern-day example of tarnishing a royal crown. One weekend while Dan and I were out having *date night*, we ran into a young couple we knew from church. Her husband held a pretty important position in his career. We both shared about our dates and where we'd been. She quickly told us they'd just finished a movie and her husband had cried through the entire thing. The look on his face as she laughed painted a clear picture of the dagger she had just driven through his heart. Men are taught to be tough and never show emotion in our culture but showing emotion with a wife should always be safe and accepted. We provide a place of refuge for their innermost thoughts and feelings. Sadly, even though we considered this couple our friends, after that conversation, he avoided us whenever he could. He had been humiliated by her sharing his vulnerability with us. It was like her waving a white surrender flag from the castle spire saying, "We surrender the kingdom." We didn't see it that way, but he did.

WHAT WILL YOU DO WITH HIS REPUTATION?

These examples show we not only hold the power to tarnish our husband's crown, but we hold his reputation in our hands. Realistically, none of us have husbands without imperfections. Women have short-comings too. Hopefully, we're all working on becoming better people as a part of our noble heritage. However, displaying our weaknesses is like hanging a sign at the gates of our kingdom inviting the enemy in. You can bet the serpent studied Adam and Eve from a distance, watching for their flaws before he curled around that tree and sold them a lie. Our duty as queen is to always uphold our husband's reputation in leadership at home, at church, in the community, and in his career, and especially to our children. So, get that polish out and remove the muck from his crown, ladies. If you've wounded him in the past, make amends, ask for forgiveness, and make a commitment to yourself and him to never sling mud in his direction again. Proverbs 31:10 says,

> *Displaying our weaknesses is like hanging a sign at the gates of our kingdom inviting the enemy in.*

Who can find a virtuous (noble) woman? For her price is far above rubies. (KJV)

As we hold their reputation in our hands, we hold responsibility to guard it well. As we build their reputation and ego, we become the priceless jewels in their crown that God created us to be.

WILL YOU GUARD THE ROYAL CHECKBOOK?

Our next *what not to do* to avoid tarnishing the crown is about managing the royal funds. This is one area women can really struggle since they're typically the ones responsible for most of the purchases made in caring for the kingdom. It's crucial we honor our husband's leadership by being self-disciplined when spending money on the groceries, clothing, etc. for the family. The nature and heart of our Abba Father is to give us more than we need like any parent desires to bless their children. Our husbands often feel the same way in their role as noble provider. Many times, they literally do want to give us the *palace*. It's woven into their nature to want to provide us with much more than our budget might even allow. We show them respect when we support and aid them to be less stressed about overspending. When we help them provide by spending wisely, they're motivated to bless us later with the things they long to give.

Many women do the household budget and bill paying because it's their strength. It's never been one of mine, but I have friends who love doing it. If that's one of your roles, my advice is to be transparent. Always gather and give to the general a financial update each month after the budget is complete. In other words, the king of your palace needs to know what's going out and what's coming in, so he can see the bigger financial picture as the general. He can't lead you into financial success if he doesn't know the details from the financial frontlines. I would also caution wives to make sure you're not hiding any of the details of your personal spending to avoid accountability. I've known women who were overspending the budget, but because they handled the finances, they never disclosed their spending. Later, they found themselves in financial ruins and the king by their side had no idea why they were in financial failure. If you want peace in the palace there must be planning for the future through financial honesty.

WILL YOU PUSH YOUR KING OUT INTO THE WILDERNESS?

Once again King Solomon has some wise advice for us to follow regarding tarnish on a royal tiara. Proverbs 21:19 challenges us not to annoy, irritate, or antagonize our husbands intentionally.

(It is) Better to live in a land of wilderness than with a wife of quarrels and provocation. (LEB)

Recently, at a marriage conference, a pastor's wife asked if I could provide an example of what this Scripture meant. She ended up providing the entire class with a great example herself. She shared how her husband hates all the decorative pillows on their bed. When she gets angry with him for any reason, she puts all those pillows on his side, so he has to move them when he comes to bed. We all had a great laugh because we could relate to her explanation. Maybe it's not pillows but something else with similar intent. I'm sure you can think of an example of something you've done to intentionally annoy your spouse. The motive is usually unresolved conflict. As women, we often want our husband's to somehow read our minds or sense why we're upset. Unlike us, men are not intuitive by nature, and they don't have that capability. Quite often they have no idea why we're acting the way we are. Let's be honest, sometimes we don't even know what's going on inside our heads. As a noble queen, we must be willing to lay down our weapons of annoyance and just be honest about how we feel. Creating conflict doesn't resolve conflict. Exasperating our husbands only adds insult to injury and that's not helping anyone accomplish anything.

Being a *royal crown* versus being a *royal pain* is a choice. The opportunity to choose is a gift from God. There are many more blessings at the palace as a result of us nobly choosing to be the jewel in our husband's crown. I'd much rather be a *diamond* than *decay* as stated in the Scripture for this chapter. When we help our king become great in the kingdom, we become the most glorious diamond atop of his head.

CROWNING POINTS

- 👑 Men have an ego that helps them rise up and lead
- 👑 You can polish his crown by showing his strengths
- 👑 Honor the royal budget and you will be blessed
- 👑 Polishing his crown elevates you to a position of beauty

Helping the king of our home elevates us to our position of splendor where we become a radiant jewel he proudly wants to display. In fact, one he would die for in order to protect. We are the crown of the kingdom! Now, let's move forward and learn the differences between the King of Hearts and the Queen of Spades!

Chapter 13

WHO IS THE QUEEN OF HEARTS AND THE KING OF SPADES?

In case you haven't noticed, men and women are about as different as the heart and spade on a deck of cards. We're similar and yet opposites. We don't look the same, we don't act the same, and we certainly don't think the same. Everything about a male and female is different. God designed us each with a distinct destiny in mind, and he called it "very good." Sadly, in the process of society defining the sexes as equal, both sexes have spiraled into an identity crisis trying to ignore the differences while trying to be the same. Men have lost touch with their strength and valor and women have determined to act tough and aggressive. Many men have fallen prey to weakness and passivity like Adam, not knowing who they are. Instead of being strong leaders, they've been conditioned to act weak and emotional which is opposite of what a queen desires. Looking at the bigger picture, it's not hard to see this is all a part of Satan's plan to disengage husbands and fathers from their role as a marriage warrior.

WHAT'S IN THE USER'S MANUAL?

Life was simpler in the days of palaces and castles. Knights had pages and squires to train in bravery for the future. Today, our husbands need to return to the warrior within them to give our sons a role model they can follow. Otherwise, we could lose an entire generation of battle-ready men. Likewise, we need to return to our true identity as women and teach our daughters who are *ladies in waiting* how to be women of dignity and poise. In days of old, when an enemy had taken territory from a kingdom, the warriors gathered their forces and took back the ground that had been stolen. This is the standard for modern-day kings and queens if we want to establish a palace plan for the future.

If we want to know who we are and why we're here, we have to go back to the source and ask the one who created us. Otherwise, we can come up with all sorts of crazy ideas about our identity and purpose. Have you noticed all the role confusion? God had specific things in mind when he created us physically, emotionally, and spiritually as man and woman different in body, mind, and soul.

WHAT'S IN YOUR DNA?

Let's consider our physical make up first. Anyone who's had high school biology might recall males and females have different DNA starting with the "X" and "Y" chromosomes. Women have two "X" chromosomes and men a "Y" and an "X" chromosome. These are the building blocks that determine all the uniqueness between the sexes. A well-known psychological study found that male and female differences show up in brains even before birth.[4]

When testosterone kicks in as the male fetus is formed inside his mother's womb, the two halves of his brain are split by a membrane, leaving only a small connection between the two parts. You can think of it as two islands with a toll bridge in between. Men tend to live on one side of their brain or the other. Most men are left-brained and operate in the realm of logic and analytical reasoning. That's what makes them great decision makers as generals on the battlefield. They can see the bigger picture and make life saving choices objectively and swiftly.

The right side of the brain houses emotions, feelings, creativity, and intuition. That's where most women tend to spend their time. It's what enables us to fill our role as the Holy Spirit and intuitively know what's happening in the heart of our kingdom day after day. It keeps us in touch with everyone's emotions. It makes us creative and helps us turn a house into a home. It's what enables us to be nurturers by nature. In women, there is no brain division that occurs in utero. Our gray matter is completely interconnected. That's why we can bounce around inside our heads from side to side like a big trampoline going from topic to topic quickly. Our thoughts can take us anywhere we want to go at any given moment.

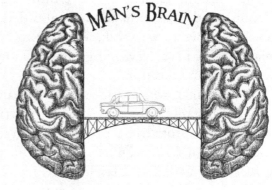

For a man to cross from one side of the brain to the other, he must first get in his car, wait in line, pay the toll, and make his way slowly across the bridge to the other side. That's why it's so difficult for most men to get in touch with their feelings. They don't want to pay the toll and do the work to cross over the bridge. If we desire for them to talk, we have to encourage them to go to the other side by loving them unconditionally while we wait patiently for them to respond.

CAN YOU PROVIDE A ROAD MAP?

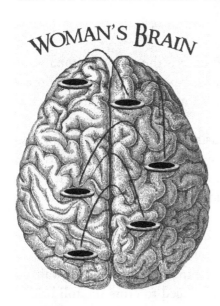

Men sometimes find it hard to follow a woman's conversation. Inevitably, men can be talking about one thing and out of the blue suddenly we can bring up something completely unrelated. At times, Dan has called a timeout to try and catch up. This physical brain difference enables a woman to recall almost anything, leaving our husbands with no idea where we are. Instantly because of the interconnections inside our head we can jump from topic to topic without skipping a beat. There's no toll bridge between our emotions and logical thought. On cue, we can bring up every detail of every conversation we've ever had. That's because we're on our trampoline bouncing wherever our thoughts take us. As a queen we can access either side of our brain simultaneously and easily overpower a man during an argument. This can translate to us overthrowing our king from his position. Because of this physical and mental difference, we have to slow down and think before we speak. We have to be willing to provide a road map, and we never leave our general at a huge disadvantage on a battlefield of communication.

Many times, when Dan and I have disagreed, I present the evidence of every instance from the past, every article I've ever read about it, and examples from five experts on why my view is correct, leaving him speechless. In reality, I'm stepping out of my responsibility to simply gather information and lay it at his feet versus do a hostile takeover of the throne. This usually generates one of three responses in a king. Either they shut down and get quiet, they quickly exit the room, or they engage to try to win the argument because they now consider us to be their enemy. We have to recognize this is all driven from innate differences between the sexes. If we work together using our strengths in unison, we all win. Remember we need their less emotional logic, and they need our quick recall and emotions to balance the situation.

WHAT'S IN THE DETAILS?

Keep in mind, this same brain difference is the reason women want to know every detail of everything that happens when we aren't present. When our husband arrives home from work or a business trip, we may find ourselves naturally wanting them to share every detail. We have to remember men are only using one side of the brain at a time to conserve brain cells, recalling only the highlights that matter to them. Details aren't important from their perspective. For us, it's how we power up our intuition. To come up with a compromise, we've had to learn to give each other space and not get angry at our differences.

Understanding differences can help us relate to one another and be more sensitive to each other's needs. Realizing men only use one side of their intellect at a time can make us more sympathetic to waiting patiently while giving them the time they need to cross the toll bridge to access their emotions. We have to also help them understand our inner need to know the details, so they can find ways to remember and share what's important for our intuitive assessment. Keep in mind this information does not give us the right to use it as an excuse for our own failures. It allows us to understand where our differences are and work to overcome them to make our relationship stronger.

WHAT'S SO CONFUSING IN THE BEDCHAMBER?

Differences between the sexes are never clearer than in the bedroom. You may have heard the expression "When it comes to sex, men are microwaves, but women are crock pots." The way men and women view sex, need sex, and desire each other are many times polar opposites. Discussing intimacy can be challenging because of varying perspectives, personal experiences, and comfort levels. In all honesty, sex is a topic we still struggle with at times, and we've been married for over three decades. Since my bachelor's degree is in health education, I've had a great deal of training in human sexuality. I want to share with you some things I've learned based on studies, personal experience, scriptural research, and more importantly—prayer.

Our sexual differences are pieces of a beautiful puzzle meant to create a work of art as they interlock.

The word cleave in Greek is the word *debaq*, which means "to glue together or to be closely joined, never to be severed." There has never been a marriage more glued together than Adam and Eve's. When God created the first man from the dust of the earth and then acknowledged his aloneness, instead of using more dirt for Eve, he formed her from the very bones of her husband. When we join together in marriage sexually, we become one flesh according to Scripture, and we're completely glued together. I believe our sexual differences are pieces of a beautiful puzzle meant to create a work of art as they interlock. They aren't meant to drive us apart. We've come to realize by working with other couples, both sexes tend to lack a scientific understanding of their bodies when it comes to human sexuality. Men are visually driven, and they tend to want what they see. Women are emotionally driven, and they usually want what they can feel. Women typically desire intimacy that is primarily tied their emotions. As you probably already know, women don't necessarily equate intimacy to the act of sex. Intimacy for us is often, but not always, about wanting to feel connected to our knight in shining armor and to feel deeply close and loved. That's why we can get as much out of snuggling and deep conversation as having sex. Men, however, don't tend to equate emotional intimacy to intercourse. They have a physical need for sexual release. Biologically, God programmed a man's body to need a sexual release about every two to three days for the typical male.

In considering our sexual contrasts, it's clear that a king and queen should use those differences to their advantage while gluing themselves together in the process. If you recall from the Venn diagrams earlier, God designed intimacy to help us become not just one in body but also one in mind and spirit. Our differences are what draw us together because opposites do attract. In science, you may recall learning how two magnets with opposite polarity attract and stick together. If their polarity is the same, they repel. That's why God created marriage between one man and one woman creating magnetism that glues us together in the bed chamber.

WHY IS THE KING FAST ASLEEP WHILE I'M WIDE AWAKE?

Scientific variables in our sexuality are visible in the hormones released in both the male and female following intercourse. Usually a woman's body responds with being energized by the hormone Oxytocin after orgasm, but the man's body responds with sleepiness and relaxation from the same hormone. We've learned to allow this to benefit us in the bedchamber. If Dan is struggling with stress and can't go to sleep, many times I graciously offer or initiate intimacy for the sake of reducing his stress level and improving his physical health. It's a lot safer than an over the counter sleep aid. Don't be disturbed if after a night-time rendezvous, you end up being wide awake. I tend to take advantage of this energy surge and get up and get something done I didn't have the time for earlier in the day. The same is true for morning bedchamber activity. If you have a busy or high-energy day ahead, the best thing for a woman is to enjoy physical time together in the morning. It will get your engine going and it's a lot healthier than a cup of high caffeinated coffee or an energy drink. Regardless of your differences, you can learn to make them work to your benefit. It's all about embracing a new perspective and allowing your hormonal challenges to work for you, and not against you.

WHAT WAS GOD THINKING?

Rest assured; God didn't wire us differently to create conflict. You may be wondering then, "Why is it so hard for us to relate and understand each other?" First, because God is a good, good Father, we can trust his plan even if it doesn't make sense to us. There are many reasons why He made us unique from one another. As James 1:2-3 proclaims,

> *Marriage isn't meant to be easy. It's meant to refine us like sandpaper and smooth out our rough edges.*

Consider it all joy, my brethren, when you encounter various trials, knowing that the testing of your faith produces endurance.

Through trials and testing, we are forced to grow and mature. Marriage isn't meant to be easy. It's meant to refine us like sandpaper and smooth out our rough edges. God loved us all too much to leave us in our own selfish state. Due to all our differences, it forces responsibility requiring us to work together to develop teamwork and perseverance. We're building a legacy and that requires cooperation. Cooperation only comes through ironing out differences in our communication and sexuality, so we become undefeatable. Secondly, if we were both exactly the same there would be no reason for one of us to exist. Our differences are one of the most important reasons God created us to be together.

CROWNING POINTS

- 👑 God created us as polar opposites for a greater purpose
- 👑 Patiently teach each other your differences to grow as one
- 👑 Allow your differences to make your marriage stronger
- 👑 Never allow differences to drive you apart

We are not complete on our own, we need each other. Women bring intuition, men bring logic. We are better together. Instead of looking at our differences as a curse, God intended them to be a blessing. When we change our perspective, it changes our mindset, and we begin to value what we have. Satan tries to use our differences to destroy us; God wants to use them to complete us. Now follow me to Chapter 14 as we dig deeper into what it means to conquer the biggest enemy at our door, the drama queen.

VICTORY

Chapter 14

WILL YOU CONQUER THE DRAMA QUEEN?

I had never seen destruction like this before. It was March 2011 when a tornado at least a mile-wide tore through the southeast destroying everything in its path. It hit my hometown leaving behind nothing but desolation. I had lived through a tornado once as a child, but the damage done then and the damage this thing brought wasn't comparable. It was impossible to comprehend unless you witnessed it firsthand.

The day after the storm hit, we contacted family members that had been in its path to see what their greatest needs were. We loaded up our car and headed there carrying water, gasoline, and financial aid. My cousin Scott, his wife Angela, and their five children barely survived the storm as it came ripping through their farm. In fact, their survival was so miraculous they ended up on the national news. They lived on twenty acres of land in a farmhouse they had built. They raised organic food and Scott owned his own construction company.

Scott had just returned home from work when he realized the sky didn't look normal. Suddenly he saw what he described as a wall of destruction headed straight for their home about a half a mile away. It wasn't a twisting, turning funnel cloud, but literally a wrecking wall a mile wide. He could hear the enormous hardwood trees ripping from the ground as the storm entered the edge of their property. He rounded up his family and began to lead them to a place of safety as fast as he could. They were headed in one direction when he heard a voice say, "Don't go to the front creek, go to the back." One stream was small and the other was deeper and wider across. The sound of the storm was deafening as he yelled to his oldest son, "Go to the back creek!"

He gathered up his five-year-old daughter who was sleeping as his wife grabbed their youngest son. They rounded up the other two boys and headed to the back riverbank.

As they got closer, they were out of time. Scott and Angela threw their children to the ground and covered them with their bodies. They had no idea where their oldest son had ended up, but they hoped he had obeyed his father. They grabbed hold of roots on the ground and hung on for what seemed like an eternity in complete darkness as they prayed for God's protection. When the storm finally passed and visibility returned, Scott began looking around to check the safety of his family. He was stunned to see the large tree that had fallen into the creek with his daughter's blanket caught in the limbs. He feared the worst. Scott hoped she hadn't been ripped out from under him by the winds. Remarkably, as he began to remove each child from the pile beneath them, he found her on the bottom fast asleep. They had all made it, but what about his oldest son? Suddenly, he popped up out of the water. He was covered in mud from head to toe, but he was alive. He had found shelter in the river under the water as he hung on to the roots of a tree for dear life.

Miraculously they all survived. When they became aware of the destruction, nothing was left except pieces of their memories. The miracle became more real when they saw the front creek-bed where they had headed first. Scott had originally run towards a metal culvert for shelter until he heard God's voice tell him to head to the back creek instead. The metal culvert was about fifteen feet in diameter, thirty feet long, and weighed thousands of pounds. Despite its size, it had been ripped from the ground by the storm. They quickly realized they all would have died had Scott not listened to the voice of his Father and obeyed. His oldest son would have also perished if he hadn't listened to his dad and gone to the back. Sometimes obedience is the difference between life and death. God prefers our obedience to his voice over everything else we have to offer him. Scott had lived his life nobly as king of his palace, and he had valiantly shown the world what a knight in shining armor is capable of when he obeys, even when it doesn't make sense. With his queen by his side, he threw his life over his family with the determination if anyone was going to perish it would have to be at the loss of his own life first.

As a result of their obedience both before and during the storm, they received an incredible blessing. God brought provision of grace in the middle of their chaos. God turned the destruction around and blessed them by doubling what they had lost. Scott and his family were handed a plantation, white columns and all at the same cost of their farmhouse. They had owned around seventeen acres and God blessed them with forty. Their farmhouse had been 2400 square feet (ca. 223 square meters) and their new home was a southern belle with 5000 square feet (ca. 465 square meters). Only God supernaturally doubles our losses.

Blessings birthed out of storms are a result of our complete obedience. As noble women, God created us to be powerful. How we use that power determines whether we exhibit the character and blessing of the Holy Spirit as a mighty rushing wind or the fury and destruction of a tornado. To win on the battlefields of life, we have to conquer our flesh and its propensity toward drama. Women are emotional beings. Our first inclination is to respond with chaotic passion when a storm is on the horizon. Had Scott's wife Angela chosen to panic in the storm, their story could have been different. Instead, she responded with diligence and peace, knowing her Father had them in his sights and her husband could be trusted.

For us to understand the weight of our choices, we're going to examine three women in Scripture who chose to be the storm versus stand in the storm with nobility. First, I'm reminded of the story of Job and his wife in the Old Testament who lost all their children when a windstorm from the desert ripped through their town. Everything they had was taken away. Job found himself in deep mourning over his losses which were compounded when he became physically ill. His life had gone from one extreme to another. He found himself with nothing but a nagging wife, a few judgmental friends, and a body full of disease. His grief was compounded by a seemingly absent God. Amid his hopelessness, his wife turned into a *drama queen*. In the middle of pandemonium, she demanded Job, "Curse God and die!" He did not take her advice. Instead, he remained faithful to God. In the end the Scripture declares that, "The Lord doubled everything that Job had once possessed." He gained everything back two-fold just as my cousin Scott and his family had.

God is faithful even in the middle of fallout from a storm. At that moment, you and I can either choose to be a *drama queen* focused on ourselves and our discomfort, or we can choose to be a queen of nobility and believe for God's faithfulness when the storms of life blow in. *Drama Queen* is defined as "a person who habitually responds to situations in a melodramatic way; a person who has exaggerated or overly emotional reactions to events or situations." Drama only adds to the tragedy in the end. We never know what we're made of until the storms come, but we can trust our God who governs the storm.

> *If our heart is beating to the drumbeat of war, conflict in the castle is prevalent.*

In all honesty, I found myself in the same situation as Job's wife while writing this book. Dan and I are currently on our own *Abraham and Sarah* journey of faith and have been for almost fifteen years. We still don't know where we're going or why God has led us to the places we've been on the journey. Neither did Abraham and Sarah. I've been very frustrated at times with wandering aimlessly in what seemed to be a *no man's land*. God moved us to the middle of nowhere at the beginning of our excursion. We have since moved again, and now recently we've realized God may be asking us to move once more. At some point we hope to be *home*.

One day while in the middle of writing this book, I was really struggling. You can bet there have been storms in my midst as I have processed grief, anger, confusion, and impatience toward God along the way. On this particular day near the beginning of our journey, I was a dramatic mess. I was observing our neighbors and feeling a little sorry for myself. I thought of how they seemed uninterested in God or faith, and yet they seemed happier than we were. Why? Satan comes to create as many storms as he can in the lives of those who've been adopted by the Father, causing them to lose hope in their identity. If we lose hope, we're no threat to his reign.

In our wilderness, I found myself saying to Dan, "Our neighbors seem happier than we do so let's just forget this journey of obedience and do what we want to. Maybe then we could actually enjoy life." This was a lie from the serpent, and I had fallen for his scheme. The truth is, turning our back on God wouldn't have brought happiness. It would have only brought emptiness. Later that same day I heard the Lord say, "You're acting like Job's wife," which was something I never expected to hear regarding myself. I was tired of waiting on the miraculous, and I wanted to sidestep God's plan by doing what seemed practical. I was saying to Dan, "Curse God and die." It was at that moment this chapter was born and I found a new source of grace for Job's wife I had never had before.

WILL YOU HELP USHER IN PEACE?

God created women to be the more sensitive, intuitive side of life as we have already learned. All these characteristics were given to us to use positively to fulfill our role as wife and mother as a reflection of the Holy Spirit. However, those same emotions can drive us to be confrontational, loud, and explosive like a hurricane creating chaos in the castle. We have to ask ourselves; will we operate in drama and usher in the storm or conquer the drama and invite peace into our midst when the storms rage?

"Happy Wife, Happy Life" is a saying I recently heard by a comedian. The audience roared, but despite its humor the laughter came because everyone in the audience knew it was true. If we're unhappy with our lives, it usually spills over into our home like a moat. It affects the other members of our family because we're the heartbeat of it all. If our heart is skipping to the right beat, we are happy and so is everyone else in the palace. If our heart is beating to the drumbeat of war, conflict in the castle is prevalent. Unfortunately, these are the circumstances that have afforded us the cultural label of being called a nag. Remember the word *nag* means to "annoy or irritate with persistent fault-finding or continuous urging." Sometimes our unhappiness is completely reasonable and our motive pure amidst the issue causing the storm. However, if we're expressing it wrongly, nobody's listening. We're nothing more than a howling wind. Regardless if the issue is valid or not, our mood sets the stage for all other moods in our domain. The wrong mood opens the door and welcomes the drama queen.

In the first book of the Bible, Genesis establishes how God created everything else in five days. Then he created Adam on the sixth day of the week. When he saw it wasn't good for him to be alone, he made Eve.

She was the last thing to stand between him and the seventh day which God called a day of rest in the creation story. Right after she came along, the next day was the Sabbath. The word *Sabbath* in Hebrew is pronounced *"Sabbat"* which means "to stop, to cease, or to keep." This is a day we're supposed to stop what we're doing, cease from working, and keep the day sacred as a day of rest.

According to Jewish tradition the woman of the home is the one who leads the opening Sabbath prayer and ushers in the ceremony of rest. Following the prayer, she lights the candle for the service. This is the personification of God's amazing design for our role as the queen of our home. We can usher in the peace of the Sabbath by shedding the light of Christ on any given circumstance in our kingdom. Not just on the Sabbath, but every day of the week. We can stop the drama and create an atmosphere of peace so our family can rest and abide. Otherwise, we can stand between our family and the Sabbath promoting foolishness with hurricane force. If we're going to succeed at being a queen of noble character, we must close the door to the hurricanes in our hearts and lead the way to the Sabbath in our homes. This is the only path to *happily ever after.*

The Bible provides another scriptural example for how we can bring peace. 1 Peter 3:4 tells us,

> *Cultivate inner beauty, the gentle, gracious kind that God delights in. The holy women of old were beautiful before God that way, and were good, loyal wives to their husbands. (MSG)*

Inner beauty comes from inner peace. Inner peace comes from abiding in God daily in every moment while conquering the drama instead of creating it. The word *abide* means to "continue without fading or getting lost." To abide in Him means to live life consistently, resting and trusting that God is God. We don't have to be a snow flurry of worry--- we can simply rest in Him every moment of every day and bring peace to our household through our example.

WHAT OTHER DRAMA QUEENS SHOULD WE REFUSE TO FOLLOW?

The first tactic of a drama queen might be leading her husband astray. Job's wife tried this tactic by pushing Job to kick God out of his life and kick the can. Eve led Adam astray by tempting him to join her and eat from the forbidden tree, causing consequences to fall upon all of mankind. As we've already learned, Sarah led her king astray by tempting Abraham to lay with her maidservant Hagar to conceive a child due to a lack of faith. Hagar gave birth to Ishmael. Abraham and Sarah's choice altered God's original plan and changed the future of the Jewish nation forever. Today they are in constant war with the nation of Palestine. Ishmael was the first-born Palestinian that today opposes Israel at the Gaza Strip. In Sarah's greed for control of the situation and her impatience to wait on God, she acted like a *drama mamma* instead of a noble queen of faith.

The good news is God used Abraham and Sarah to fulfill his plans regardless of the disobedient whirlwind affair. God can still use us even if we've previously led our husband astray. We can be encouraged that we don't have to walk under the attitudes and influence of the *drama queen* mentality. It is never too late to change. God's grace is big enough to keep us from leading our husbands awry or making our own way when we get impatient with God. He is trustworthy and faithful even when we make huge mistakes. All we have to do is trust him with our past and our future.

WHO WERE THE HEAVYWEIGHT DRAMA QUEENS OF OLD?

Two powerful women in Scripture come to mind when I think of double drama. The first was the *queen* of all drama queens. Her name was Jezebel, and many theologians consider her to be at the top of the chain of Satan's command of dramatic chaos in our world today. You can read about her in 1st & 2nd Kings in the Old Testament of the Bible. She was a queen and prostitute; she was a woman of vulgarity and sexual exploits. She used a spirit of fear and intimidation to control those she wanted to rule. She emasculated her husband, creating a coward who couldn't lead. She had castrated male eunuchs who answered to her beckoned calls. She robbed others to please her own desires and killed to get what she wanted. She worshiped the false god Baal, holding orgies in the temple to celebrate fertility in his honor. When a baby was born as a result of an orgy, they sacrificed it on an altar as an act of worship. She used her royal influence to lead other women into iniquity by murdering their children.

Another drama queen in Scripture whom I would consider second in command to Jezebel was Delilah. She exhibited many of the same characteristics as her counterpart. She and her male companion were known as *Samson and Delilah*. You can find their account in Judges 16 of the Old Testament. Samson was a gift from God to his parents because his mother was barren. God had great plans for his life as a judge over the Israelites, but he was to keep the Nazirite vow. The word *Nazir* in Hebrew means "to be separated or consecrated." It meant he was to be set apart for a specific time period by following a set of rules. Samson was to abstain from cutting his hair for the duration of the vow because his uncut hair gave him superhuman strength. Instead of living a life of purity, Samson halfheartedly kept his vows choosing instead to live by complete and utter chaos. He was a powerful young man but a disobedient son who liked the ladies so much that women were his greatest weakness. Eventually, one of his pursuits dealt him a whole lot of drama and destruction. She was the woman of Sorek named Delilah.

Samson first married a Philistine woman against his parent's wishes. The Philistines were the enemies of God's people. After the wedding, his wife was tragically murdered as a result of his ongoing battle with her people. When Samson met Delilah, he was on the rebound from her death. He was captivated and fell prey to Delilah's seductive ways. She loved money more than she loved him, and as the Philistines plotted to destroy Samson, they offered her eleven-hundred shekels in exchange for his life. All Delilah had to do was provide the secret to Samson's strength. She agreed and got busy taunting him to discover the answer to the mystery. Samson played along with her games not realizing the danger. She eventually wore him down with her nagging until he became "sick to death of it." In frustration, he told her his strength was in his uncut hair. When he fell asleep that night, Delilah lopped off his braids. The Philistines rushed in, taking him prisoner. They mercilessly tortured him, gouged out his eyes, and threw him in prison. As a grand finale' to his tragic life, Samson conquered the drama with his own theatrical ending. With three thousand Philistines watching, he begged God to restore his strength. Then he mustered up the energy and pressed against the columns of the building yelling, "Let me die with the Philistines." The entire temple collapsed killing Samson along with everyone present. Instantly, he killed more Philistines in dying than while he was alive.

In looking at Jezebel's and Delilah's traits, many were the same but operated a little different in each of their stories. They both used their beauty and seductive sexual ways to get what they wanted. They both emasculated the men in their lives. They both loved money and coveted or stole what they desired from the people in their path. Instead of stealing as Jezebel did, Delilah took bribes in exchange for secrets. Both women had no respect for men. These women wielded a spirit of fear and hopelessness to control and manipulate, leading to the humiliation and sometimes the death of their victims.

The spirit of Jezebel and Delilah are visible in our culture today, and they wield their powerful weapons to create a veil of depression, hopelessness, and self-destruction over our world. Today, America is facing the highest level of suicide rates since the Great Depression. The real question in this chapter is, "Will we take our authority over the drama that surrounds us and stop it before it destroys us and the men we love?". We have to learn to recognize the characteristics of these spirits if we're going to destroy them. Jezebel and Delilah are evident in the pornography that is rapidly infiltrating the minds of our husbands, sons, and fathers. They can be seen in the thievery and greed that's going on in the world around us. In Revelation, the last book of the Bible which is an account of our future, Jezebel is mentioned, and we are told that witchcraft will deceive the nations of the world. The word *witchcraft* in Greek is the word "pharmakeia". Jezebel and Delilah in their transfixing way can be seen in the opioid crisis and the pharmaceutical drug companies peddling chemicals versus health. They're in the media portraying parents as unimportant and out of touch representing the *father* persona as weak and ignorant, and the mother as domineering and emasculating. They're in an educational system that teaches sex of any kind is acceptable while failing to warn of the damage that sex outside of marriage can do. They're in the abortion industry deceiving women into sacrificing their children on an altar of greed. It's clear in the determined destruction of the church by the propaganda against religious rights. It's in the judges rewriting law from the bench instead of ruling on its constitutionality with objectivity.

WHERE DO I FIND THE COURAGE TO STOP THE STORM?

As in the story of the Prophet Elijah, who confronted Jezebel, our position as believers in Christ is no longer respected. Our dignity has been stepped on, and our destiny is in danger. These destructive issues and the role they have played in radically changing culture can be seen in the timeline of history and the events unfolding before our eyes. We cannot allow ourselves to be blinded by their deception any longer. We have to open our eyes to the truth to stop the dramatic demolition of marriage as daughters of the King and queens of our kingdom. We can use the power of God's love to turn our lives around and conquer our past and walk victoriously into our future. Let me encourage you with an amazing biblical account from Scripture that went from dramatic failure to forgiven. Unlike Jezebel and Delilah, it didn't end in tragedy. We can learn from her turnaround, miracles are possible. All it takes is a little courage from you and me. Our courage to destroy the power of *Jezebels* and *Delilahs* must come from our Father in Heaven.

Bathsheba was another *drama queen* who also became a bride of King David, but her story ended in restoration. Her saga began one night when David stayed home from a battle to get some rest and relaxation at the palace. As he stargazed from the balcony, his eyes fell upon a beauty queen bathing naked on the rooftop of a chaotic villa down below. He was overtaken with lust and determined to have Bathsheba as his own. He sent his servant to bring her to his bed chamber. In one night, David turned his peaceful palace into a chaotic castle with forbidden passion. In the heat of the moment Bathsheba got pregnant. As a result of his guilt, he sent her husband to the frontlines of the battlefield where he was killed. King David then took Bathsheba to be his wife and the child that she was carrying died a tragic death. Talk about drama at the royal residence.

The spirit of Jezebel can lead a great and noble warrior into adultery. I'm sure Bathsheba was honored to be in the bed chamber of the brave and noble King David. So much so, that she left the covenant of her marriage behind, leaving a hailstorm in her wake. David and Bathsheba had no idea their one night of passion would lead to years of chaotic catastrophes.

WHAT HAPPENS WHEN THE DRAMA QUEEN ENTERS THE STAGE?

The royal couple's choices affected their children and future on a hurricane level. David's son, Amnon, raped his own sister Tamar by deceiving her and pretending to be ill. He saw something he wanted sexually, just as his father had, and he set out to take it. Absalom her full brother, begged his father to avenge his sister's rape, but he refused. Out of anger, Absalom hunted Amnon down himself and killed him. Absalom lost respect for his father and as a result of his anger he tried to have King David murdered to overthrow the throne. He, too, had seen something he wanted and set out to take it. These children of the king all lost their lives tragically because of the choices their father had made. Are you starting to see the patterns that are unleashed when we walk under the deception of these evil spirits? It's like throwing a rock in the castle moat and watching the ripple effect reach the next generation. This family was ravaged through greed, rape, murder, covetousness, and treason. As it wreaked havoc on the family, the peaceful palace was no more.

There's always a risk of casualties in the kingdom when the Jezebels and Delilahs show up on our doorsteps.

I've seen the chaos the spirit of Jezebel and Delilah have brought into the lives of women I've coached in crisis. When we fail to raise the draw bridge and let the drama queens in, they seek to destroy the king and queen of the palace through the weapons they wield. I began to see a pattern. As I coached a young woman, she mentioned her children had recently both been injured in separate car accidents a week apart as she expressed suspicion of her husband committing adultery. I knew from experience, if he's entertaining a drama queen there can sometimes be a trickle-down effect as with King David and Bathsheba. I knew if her children were experiencing chaos there could be a storm brewing. When she confronted her husband, he admitted his guilt.

In another instance, a woman, whose husband had just walked out claiming to be in love with his secretary, found herself in a hospital by her son's bed. He had been injured in an accident requiring his foot to be amputated. The storm around her castle wreaked havoc on her children. In another circumstance, a woman victimized by adultery had a daughter who was assaulted and barely escaped being raped. There's always a risk of casualties in the kingdom when the Jezebels and Delilahs show up on our doorsteps.

The chaos these spirits bring doesn't just come in the form of possible risks to the children either. After separation or divorce many couples find themselves financially devastated as if Jezebel was robbing them blind or Delilah was selling their secrets. I don't want to misguide you so let me make this clear. Not every financial challenge or injury to a child is related to sexual misconduct by a spouse. It's the exception and not the rule; otherwise we could find ourselves living under the spirit of fear. However, we must realize when the drama queen spirit does enter our life it will wreak havoc on our children and our finances every time. They often bring hopelessness, depression, and, yes, even suicidal thoughts. If we are experiencing any of these kinds of circumstances we must step back and pray for wisdom and discernment, letting our Father give us his perspective and the weapons to defeat them.

WILL YOU CONQUER THE DRAMA THAT'S HEADED YOUR WAY?

The weapon for winning the battle over the drama queen is easier to defeat than you might think. The key is in our adoption. God adopts us and then calls us to be the "salt and light" of the world; the salt that heals and cures and the light that shines its love for the world to see. According to NASA's reports the highest level of saltiness that exists is found right in the center of a peaceful ocean. According to this same study, the least amount of saltiness in the ocean is found where the storms rage and there is no evaporation. We cannot evaporate goodness out into culture if we're living right in the middle of the storm. Living in the storm causes us to lose our saltiness. How do we stop the dramatic tempest threatening to destroy us? By living our lives right in the middle of the living water of Christ, radiating his love out onto the people surrounding us who do not know him. It starts first with our determination to finish the race of marriage well. To redo and remake our homes into the homes they were meant to be, we have to work alongside our knight in shining armor with the King of all Kings. We have a responsibility to examine every area of our life and allow the Father to examine every area of our heart, so we can straighten our crown and live our best life.

Because of our intuitive nature, we are usually more comfortable asking the tough questions. Are we leading our king astray like Eve did? Are we emasculating him like Jezebel did? Are we contemptuous toward our spouse like Delilah was? Do we speak words of death or life over our household? Do we use our influence to gossip, ridicule, or maliciously slander others? Next, are we coveting our neighbor's things so much that we're leaving our family behind in the dust as we pursue our dreams without any regard for their well-being?

To rearrange and change our level of drama, we have to grow and strengthen our relationship with our Father first. Are we turning a deaf ear to the gospel of Jesus and his Word because we love ourselves more than we love his sacrifice to save us? Are we rebellious against the laws and guidelines meant to govern us or the biblical principles meant to teach us? These are tough things to answer but if we're going to rise above the moat that threatens to overflow into our future, we must be strong enough to face the internal storm. If you answered "yes" to any of the questions above, then you have some palace cleanup to do. It's never too late for God to intervene on your behalf!

IS THERE HOPE AFTER DRAMA?

The most exciting and encouraging news about this chapter is God brings hope into all hopeless situations when we ask for his forgiveness! God's ability to restore, renew, and remake us is ever-present, and he is always ready to step in if we'll only ask. In the case of Abraham and Sarah, their promised son Isaac became the ancestor of King David. David was a direct forefather in the bloodline of Jesus. God kept his promise, and they rose above the chaos they had created. In the account of King David and Bathsheba's adultery, God restored his kingdom back to order despite the lasting effects of some of his choices. Ephesians 3:20 declares,

*Now to him who is able to do immeasurably more than all we ask
or imagine, according to his power that is at work within us.*

Soon after David's marriage to Bathsheba, David was confronted by
the prophet Nathan about his adultery. Nathan faced the risk of death
by reprimanding the king, but he chose obedience over fear. David
bravely made no excuses. He did not blame Bathsheba as Adam did
with Eve. Instead, he chose to embrace responsibility as a noble king
should and confess his mistake. He repented, receiving God's mercy
and forgiveness! We can respond the same way when confronting the
truth. 1 Samuel 12:13b shows that God's mercy covered David's failure
in Nathan's response,

The Lord has taken away your sin and you are not going to die.

—⁓⁓—
*The choice of living life
like a drama queen or
conquering drama like a
noble queen is up to us!*
—⁓⁓—

Regardless of the scars, David was
restored to royal favor by God's grace. We
aren't told what happened to Bathsheba
once the confession and repentance of
David was complete. However, we can
look in Scripture for the trail she left
behind. We see the first evidence of her
life change when God granted them another son, and they named
him Solomon which means *"beloved of the Lord."* We also know that
Solomon was given the throne upon his father's death. Bathsheba was a
Godly mother who raised her son well because as we have discovered in
the pages of this book, Solomon is considered the wisest king in Bible
history. Most importantly, Bathsheba went on to be in the ancestral
bloodline of Christ as Matthew 1 tells us,

*...she was restored to divine favor, and now virtuous and wise as
well as beautiful, she raised Solomon in Godly diligence and care.*

Finally, one of the most compelling evidences of God's power to
restore us from drama is in one of Solomon's writings. Many theologians give Bathsheba credit as being the Proverbs 31 woman which is
the model many of us aspire to be as strong, noble wives. If you've never

read it, go to Proverbs 31 to see what a powerful Godly woman is supposed to be based on Bathsheba's example.

King David and Bathsheba's story is exciting news for us all! No matter what we have done or how much *drama queen* we may have played on the stage of our castle, we can leave it all behind and let the curtain fall! The choice of living life like a drama queen or conquering drama like a noble queen is up to us!

CROWNING POINTS

- 👑 Choose to be a noble queen not a drama momma
- 👑 When things get hard don't betray your faith
- 👑 Unlike Jezebel or Delilah, don't lead your husband astray
- 👑 Be prepared to armor up if drama shows up unannounced
- 👑 Your past does not have to dictate your future

Wow, we are just one chapter away from conquering the chaos for good. Follow me as we learn how to dine at the King's table and reap the rewards for a lifetime!

Chapter 15

WILL YOU SIT AT THE KING'S TABLE?

In this chapter we're taking a totally different approach. We shift our perspective to the only King that holds the power to change our chaotic castle into a peaceful palace once and for all. It makes sense that we should end where everything began, by dealing with our relationship to our Heavenly Father as the King of all Kings. Our primary role as his bride and the queen of our kingdom gives us the power to change the world when we pray.

Let's explore what it looks like to sit at the table of our Father and openly express our needs. The outcome of our conversation is based on our willingness to petition the King of our heart for the salvation and deliverance of our family out of the grip of the enemy's hands. At this table we can make a plea for our husband's character, his destiny as a noble leader, and the future of our children. James 5:16 promises us,

The earnest prayer of a righteous person has great power and produces wonderful results. (NLT)

WHAT'S AN ALLEGORY?

We have explored Queen Esther's life from different perspectives in the pages of this book. She was a noble queen who lived upright. She's been a role model for us on many levels. This queen was destined to save not just her family, but an entire race of people through bravery and obedience. She stood against an enemy who was determined to destroy everyone she held dear. Once again, we can benefit from the

Queen of Persia by considering her love story from a new angle. This time, we're going to use her narrative as an allegory to discover what she did to save her people, so we can save ours. An *allegory* is defined as a "metaphor or a parallel used to reveal a hidden moral." Esther's model can change how we view our prayers as a wife with power and purpose. She approached the King on a mission to stop the enemy in his tracks.

Before we jump in, I want to lay out each character in her story so the metaphor will be easier to understand. First, imagine you are Esther in this storyline. You are a beautiful, adorned queen who lives in a palace. You have an appointed destiny and a lot of power and it's time to recognize it and step into it.

In Esther's story, Mordecai was a leader of the Jewish people and became her adoptive father when her parents were killed. At some point Mordecai had even exposed a conspiracy of treason against King Xerxes keeping the King from being murdered. Mordecai wanted what was best for the entire kingdom, and he willingly put his life at risk to expose the treasonous plot. He was also head of her family. In this allegory he represents the head of our home. This kind of leadership, along with his bravery, is the characteristics we long for in our husband. The Jewish people in this chapter will represent your family. They were dependent on Esther's obedience, and they needed her to intervene on their behalf. This is what our children need from us for their future to be secured.

In our allegory, King Xerxes will represent the true King of our lives and the King of all Kings, our Heavenly Father. King Xerxes oversaw the entire kingdom. He waged war against the enemies of his day, putting his life on the line for the sake of saving the domain he ruled. This is what our Father does for us daily. This is why Jesus died. The enemy in this chapter is Haman. He was an angry Amalekite who hated God's children. He worked his way up inside the ranks and positioned himself near the throne. King Xerxes had appointed him a powerful position and Haman intended to use it to destroy the Jewish race. In our allegory, Haman represents our greatest enemy, Satan. He himself was appointed a powerful position but after failing to overthrow the King of Heaven, he now seeks to destroy and overthrow us. Just as Haman falsely accused the Jews to the king, Satan stands in accusation against us daily at the throne of God, calling us unworthy. As we move through this chapter, remember the characters in the storyline and who they represent. It will make the message and our mandate of going to the King's table for conversation much easier to understand.

WILL YOU OBEY NO MATTER WHAT IT COSTS?

It was the middle of the night. I was restless and couldn't sleep. As I went to get a drink of water, suddenly I heard that familiar voice in my head clearly speak to me saying, "You are moving." I was half asleep and totally convinced I must have been hearing things. Of course, God doesn't speak in an audible voice, but it was as if He were yelling in my mind. He spoke again saying, "No, you are moving!" It was so overwhelming it literally took my breath away. I immediately went into my closet to keep from waking Dan and began to pray and argue with God. A few hours later, I stood knowing we were in fact moving. I was not to speak of it until the Lord prepared Dan's heart for what was about to take place. Why would I dare argue with God? He had been right every other time he'd spoken throughout my life. However, as queen of my palace, I liked where we lived and had no desire to leave. We were in a house we had completely remodeled and in a church where we had served for almost fifteen years. We had a flourishing ministry we had built from the ground up. It was a comfortable existence where we wanted to stay until our children finished school.

Suddenly, in just one night everything about our life and future changed just as it had for Esther. She found herself swept up and carried away to a new unfamiliar place in the king's kingdom. She had been orphaned and then adopted by her Uncle Mordecai's family. They lived in the countryside in a comfortable community with other Jews. One night the foot soldiers of King Xerxes showed up with a command to gather all the young, fair maidens and bring them to the castle. They would be prepared and pampered until the king chose one of them to become the new queen by his side. The King had beckoned, and Esther had to obey. Against her wishes, she had to go where the king said go and wait for her destiny to unfold. Just like us, it would cost her everything she had known.

When God said move, Esther had no choice and neither did we. We put our house up for sale, and in a few short months, we had a contract on it. We had twenty days to figure out where we were going. We felt led to a new town about fifty miles away. It wasn't clear what God had planned. He did make us some specific promises about the reason for our journey, but we had no idea when or how those promises would come to pass. We hung onto those commitments in the dark hours of waiting and wondering. I imagine Esther did the same thing as she held to her heritage as a Jew. In the dark hours of uncertainty, she pondered her fate. For many months, she was prepped and pampered while wondering what the future would bring. I understood her circumstances. God had swept us away to the unknown against our desires. We, too, knew our destiny was attached to the move.

Just as Esther hung on to hope, we've hung on knowing and believing that God keeps his promises, and we can trust our destiny in his hands. We recognized it was a season of preparation. Esther was in the same season after her relocation. She was being pampered and prepared to meet the King. Even though she was experiencing spa treatments befitting a queen, it's doubtful she enjoyed them all. She was probably more worried about her future than the present moment. In our journey to the unknown, we trusted God while struggling to relish the experience of our new location with overwhelming uncertainty. God moved us away from friends and family. He shook us loose from some of our misguided beliefs and gave us new understanding about the power of the Holy Spirit in our personal lives. He washed away things that weren't pleasing like religiosity. Our Father refined us like a fire burning away things that weren't noble. Then he restored us and delivered us from our past bringing complete inner healing. It was excruciatingly painful and yet wonderful all at the same time. I imagine Esther must have felt the same way as the king's maidservants scrubbed away her blemishes and washed away her countryside dirt to prepare her for an appointment with the King.

At the close of our fifth year in our new location, God began to show us our wandering in the wilderness was moving us once again. We believed whatever God was doing had to do with fulfilling the promises he made at the beginning. As we pondered the possibility of relocating again, I joined a women's Bible study called *Esther-It's Tough Being a Woman*[5] by Beth Moore. I was in the middle of writing this book. One night in my studies, I recognized what I believed to be a profound discovery that could apply to every wife in her role as queen of her home. Esther's story was an allegory to ours as the queen of our household. My newfound revelation totally changed my perspective on the power we have in determining our husband's destiny and our family's future, and this chapter was born.

WILL YOU CHOOSE TO BE A QUEEN ESTHER?

The theme of this book refers to husbands and wives and the royal position we hold as redeemed children of God. Esther's example gives us insight on how to live in that position with poise. She became the bride of the King of Persia over all the other maidens gathered from the countryside. She had been thrust into position as archduchess through a whirlwind marriage. She was given a seat at his royal table. Like her, we're given a seat at the Lords table as adopted children through our marriage to the bride groom, Jesus. Our faith thrusts us into a new position of authority.

Just like Esther, we suddenly find a new identity, and we're transformed instantaneously into nobility. As children of the King, we're given a seat at the Lord's table through our adoption. As a part of that relationship, we gain an incredible position of influence in the destiny of our family. Like the new Queen of Persia, we have the ear of the King and play an important role in saving our family and their future.

When Haman entered the stage representing our enemy, he was the right-hand man to the king. He deceived Xerxes into making a decree that all the Jews should be killed on a particular day on the Jewish calendar. He convinced the king they were worthless to his kingdom. The king didn't know his new bride was also a Jew since she had been brought to the palace by his foot soldiers. When Mordecai heard of the new decree, he sent word telling Esther the Jews would be killed unless she intervened. He reminded her that she had gained position for a purpose and the salvation of her bloodline was up to her. In Esther 4:14b Mordecai speaks saying,

And who knows but that you have come to royal position for such a time as this? Esther 4:14

When our family's salvation or safety is at risk it's a serious matter. You may have been chosen to be the queen of your palace for such a time as this. Your husband's salvation might rest on your petition at the King's table. The Bible teaches in I Peter 3:1-2 and 4 that a wife can lead her husband to the Lord with a quiet and gentle spirit.

Wives, in a similar way, place yourselves under your husband's authority. Some husbands may not obey God's word. Their wives could win these men (for Christ) by the way they live without saying anything. (GWT)

We can drive our husband away from the Lord by speaking our minds about his condition instead of speaking directly to the King of Kings. We don't have to petition our husbands for a change of heart; instead, we can take our request straight to the throne room and sit at the royal table like Esther. If you're married to a warrior who doesn't believe or have a strong relationship with the Father, you must realize the seriousness of his fate. He's at risk of losing his soul or never walking into his potential as the knight in shining armor you long for him to be. It's the most serious matter involved in your future as well as your household's.

HOW DO WE PREPARE TO ENTER THE KING'S PRESENCE?

Queen Esther realized the seriousness of her mission. As we've discussed, she fasted and prayed for three days. According to Biblical meaning, the number *three* is "that which is solid, real, substantial, complete, and entire." She took the time to get her thoughts together.

Our need is real, and our petition for the Father's help is complete when we walk forward into his presence.

When her faith was solid, she was ready to approach the throne room. Her concerns were real, her authority in God was substantial, and her plan was complete. Her new position had been planned for this moment, and her family's future hung in the balance.

Anytime we go to the King's table to present our petition we must prepare. We can apply the method she used to our lives as well. First, we equip our hearts. We fast and pray if necessary. We stand on our faith. Then we walk forward in our authority as the bride, knowing our title is substantial enough to give us opportunity to be heard by the King of Kings. Our need is real, and our petition for the Father's help is complete when we walk forward into his presence. We can take our seat at the King's table for a frank conversation on our family's behalf.

WILL YOU WEAR A ROYAL ROBE AND APPROACH THE THRONE?

As Esther prepared to go before the king, she cleansed herself and bathed in fragrant perfume to appear before the royal court. We too can be cleansed with the fragrance of royalty. Scripture teaches us through the cleansing blood of Jesus we're washed whiter than snow from all our unrighteousness through confession and repentance. We confess our failures; receive his forgiveness and are covered in a new garment. He wraps us in a robe of righteousness, and we're draped in a new identity as the bride to the King, as stated in Isaiah 1:18,

> *"Come now, let us settle the matter," says the Lord. "Though your sins are like scarlet, they shall be as white as snow; though they are red as crimson, they shall be like wool."*

The blood shed on the cross on our behalf covers our life like a royal robe as Isaiah 61:10 reveals,

> *I delight greatly in the Lord; my soul rejoices in my God. For he has clothed me with garments of salvation and arrayed me in a robe of his righteousness, as a bridegroom adorns his head like a priest, and as a bride adorns herself with her jewels.*

HAS THE SCEPTER BEEN EXTENDED TO ME?

Within Persian rule, it was illegal for a person to approach the king without the presentation of a summons. Therefore, approaching the throne was not to be taken lightly. To enter without invitation was an act of treason, even for the queen of the palace. Upon approach, if the king showed favor and extended his golden scepter, the person would be pardoned. Except for this, the law would have demanded Esther be killed. As she approached King Xerxes with a heart of humility, understanding her position, she hoped to find favor from the king. She prayed her life would be spared. Esther 4:16b portrays the bravery she showed at the risk of death,

I will go to the King, even though it is against the law. And if I perish, I perish.

Scripture teaches us we can approach the throne of God with the same heart as Esther. Our King in Heaven cares for us, and he is interested in the petitions we bring before him as a member of his royal bloodline. I Pet. 5:6-7 proclaims,

Humble yourselves, therefore, under God's mighty hand, that he may lift you up in due time. Cast all your anxiety on him because he cares for you.

Just as Esther willingly laid down her life for her family and the Jewish nation, we can do the same. She went courageously, showing humility and understanding due the position of the king. We can go to the throne in boldness on our family's behalf, while showing the King of Kings the honor he deserves.

As a result of her honor the king received her and pardoned her by extending his royal scepter. He gave her the opportunity to be heard. Unlike Esther, we don't have to fear for our life when we go to the King. There is no risk of being condemned. Jesus died to make a way for us to approach the throne of Heaven. In the days of castles and kings, the *scepter* was "an ornamental staff carried by rulers on ceremonial occasions as a symbol of sovereignty." The King of Kings extended his golden scepter down to us when He extended his son down to us on the cross. When he presented Jesus, he was granting us favor. We can now approach the throne without being afraid and receive love and acceptance. We don't step into God's presence in fright, but with rejoicing. Unlike Esther's circumstances where risk was involved, there is no risk for us. The only risk to us is if we never choose to go. Hebrews 4:16 states,

Let us therefore come boldly to the throne of grace, that we may obtain mercy and find grace to help (us) in time of need. (NKJV)

ARE YOU WILLING TO GO TO THE TABLE AND CONFRONT THE ENEMY?

Once Esther entered the throne room and the scepter was extended, she began putting her plan into action. First, she invited the king and Haman to dinner. He accepted her invitation to sit at the table and feast. As the queen of our palace, our King in heaven wants us to break bread with him by feasting on his Word daily. We have the opportunity to converse with him freely about our kingdom's affairs and dine with him over his Scripture.

Our journey to the King's table is not just about salvation. It's also about defeating the enemy and crushing his attacks against our kingdom. As the bride of Christ, we can make our requests known and trust him to give us victory in our battles. We especially need to petition our Father on our husband's behalf for any just cause benefiting him or our family. Our husband is at the top of the chain of command in our palace, and when his life is in order everyone's life underneath him falls into place. 1 Peter 5:6-7 challenges us with these words when we approach the King,

> *So, humble yourselves, therefore, under the mighty power of God, and at the right time he will lift you up in honor. Give your worries and cares to God, for he cares about you. (NLT)*

The salvation of the Jews depended on Esther's petition to the king and her willingness to confront her enemy in his presence. She knew her enemy and had no choice but to face Haman when the time came. We must do the same thing when Satan is in our midst. Our husband's life, career, destiny, or future may depend on it. Our children's hope may rely on it. By entering our Father's presence, and breaking bread with Him through prayer, we face our enemy. Just like Esther, we can gather and present the evidence to the King, defining the threat the enemy brings through his false accusations. Satan falsely accuses us as he stands at the throne of our God. In Luke 22:31 Jesus gives insight to the nature of his accusations when speaking to his disciple Simon Peter. He implies our accuser enters the throne of God and asks for permission to persecute us.

Simon, Simon, look out! Satan has asked to sift you like wheat. Luke 22:31 (Holman)

In Job, we see another reference to the enemy as our accuser.

One day the members of the heavenly court came again to present themselves before the Lord, and the Accuser, Satan, came with them. Job 2:1 (NLT)

Our enemy is daily plotting for our demise just like Haman plotted against the Jews. That's why God sent his son, Jesus, to die on our behalf. Jesus is now the defender of our faith. Following his resurrection, he returned to Heaven and took his place at the right hand of the throne. Jesus stands to defend us against the enemy's lies and accusations. He speaks to God Almighty as our defense attorney. Satan makes accusations as the prosecuting attorney. We are declared innocent when we accept the gift of Jesus' defense by choosing to be adopted into the royal family. Satan now has no evidence to present in his case. They are all false accusations because of Jesus' blood. Just like Esther, we know the truth, and we too can faithfully stand on the facts, knowing our King will pardon our family.

WHAT DO YOU REALLY WANT?

Esther knew she had the king's favor when he extended the scepter. She then moved forward to confront the enemy, hoping the King of Persia might help her save the Jews. Esther chose to have dinner with the king twice. We can go to the King of Kings more than once to make our requests known. In fact, according to Luke 18:7, he wants us to come repeatedly until our prayers are answered.

And will not God bring about justice for his chosen ones, who cry out to him day and night? Will he keep putting them off?

At the second dinner, Esther boldly embraced her destiny as queen, doing her part to petition the king for justice. After she revealed the evidence against Haman, King Xerxes realized how his officer had deceived him. The king immediately ordered Haman hung on the gallows that he had ordered built just days before as he planned for Mordecai's death.

Our King in Heaven, who is also Judge, desires for us to sit down and take our rightful place as his bride at the table. He has destined us to speak boldly on our family's behalf, putting the enemy in his rightful place! When I began to see the correlations between Esther's story and its relevance to our role as wives, my eyes were opened to the real potential we have to stop the adversary and put our kingdom in order. The death meant for us is now meant for Satan.

WHAT HAPPENS WHEN THE ENEMY IS DEFEATED?

When Esther presented her case and defeated her enemy, Mordecai was given passage to his destiny. The King brought him into the palace, making him second only to himself in royal position. Then he placed a robe on his back and a signet ring on his finger. Historically, the *signet ring* of the king was "a symbol of authority and honor to the nobleman who wore it." It bore the emblem unique to that particular king giving the ring bearer the right to make decisions and decrees on the king's behalf. They were legitimate proclamations representing the king's endorsement.

Don't we want our husband to bear the signature of the King of Kings? As the queen of our palace, is it not our heart's desire for our nobleman to walk in authority over our household, making decisions for our Father in Heaven who is King? If our husband wears the signet ring of the King, every fear we have about our future is dismantled. Symbolically, we place the ring on our husband's finger in our wedding ceremony as a representation of his authority to lead our home well as ambassador to the King.

Interestingly enough, after Esther's plan was complete and the Jews lives were spared, she isn't mentioned again in the remainder of the book that bears her name. Instead, the rest of the Biblical account is about Mordecai and all that he accomplished. In his honored position as the king's right-hand man, he changed culture and saved a nation. This is God's glorious design for marriage. Everything in our palace is placed in order when our husband steps into his position, second only to the King of Glory making him an amazing leader and protector.

WILL YOU STEP ASIDE?

Esther's role in the narrative was that of a heroin saving her family from harm. She was neither self-seeking nor motivated by her desires. She was not interested in claiming her place of fame in the kingdom. She simply aided in making sure justice was served and the head of her home stood in his rightful position. There's lesson here for us as wives. We can view our role with a new perspective. We have a call on our lives to do great things, but the first order of business for the queen is to do the thing that makes our family safe and moves our husband into his rightful place as leader and nobleman, second only to the Commander in Chief. As a result, we put the enemy on the gallows to hang.

The one crown we can never wear successfully is the crown meant to be worn on our husband's head.

Many couples have lived their lives in chaos versus peace as this concept has been overlooked. Women can wear many *crowns* in walking out their role, but the one crown we can never wear successfully is the crown meant to be worn on our husband's head. It will never fit us. In truth, I'm sometimes tempted to try on my husband's crown. One of the hardest things to conquer in ourselves is the inner strength God gave us as women. It was given to us by our Creator with his destiny for us in mind, but the resilience we have has to be channeled in a divine direction. It takes true royal grit as the queen of our palace to channel our strength in the right manner rather than pull away from our identity and stand independently strong. God created women to be powerful while donning the only crown we were meant to wear. That of a beautiful queen.

This was Eve's problem when she made the choice to eat from the forbidden tree. She was created to fill Adam's emptiness and use her strength to help him walk out his created purpose. Fulfilling her role would have given her freedom to boldly walk out her own. Unfortunately, she pulled away and independently took a bite of forbidden royal fruit, altering God's original plan.

Many of us have done the same thing. Unfortunately, this leads to the loss of blessing that the King of Kings means for us to have as wives. I could name a number of couples who are unhappy for this reason. The faces are different, but the stories are all the same. A husband has a clear purpose, career, or call on his life; yet his wife has decided her destiny is much more important than his or that his dreams won't provide for the things she longs to have in her royal residence. As a result, her husband never settles into a palace of contentment and the wife is always unhappy because whatever he does is never enough. There is no peace without a palace, and they are left with a war torn, chaotic castle of discontentment. He will probably never reach his destiny, and neither will she. The worst part is how their choices will also affect their children. That is not to say that once their children are adults, they won't be able to overcome their restless past, but many times they only grow up to repeat it.

Esther could have loved her position more than she loved her people and ignored the decree of her king out of fear or selfish motive. Instead, she boldly walked to the front of the palace with a plan in place to save a nation. As strong women with powerful positions, we must lay our lofty ambitions to rest and pursue what is best for the kingdom. In doing so, we will gain our rightful place as a queen with a purpose. The Bible declares when we lay down our life, we actually find it.

WHAT'S MY REAL PURPOSE?

God's word teaches us that each life has a purpose. What I didn't realize was the first part of my purpose as the queen of my palace is to stand under and hold up my husband in prayer and do my best to help him succeed at whatever God has created him to do. As I researched for this book, I was relieved to discover that the grocery list culture has handed us about our role is not actually real. It will never fulfill us or make us happy.

For years, women have chosen to sit at the world's kitchen table trying to be all things to all people instead of sitting at God's banquet table as the beautiful queen we were created to be. We've played the roles of a loving wife, a mother, a taxicab driver, a baseball coach, soccer mom, Girl Scout cookie peddler, nurse, therapist, a short-order cook, a lingerie model, a career-loving corporate-ladder climbing female, and even the Suzie-Do-Good at church, all in pursuit of happiness. I can relate to that list. I've been a wife for thirty years, a mother for twenty-five, and a home-school teacher for twenty. I've owned my own business, held a dozen church positions as a children's choir coordinator, music-drama evangelist, songwriter, marriage conference speaker, premarital coach, and a college professor, all while trying to fulfill my role as queen of the palace. You probably have your own overwhelming list. I don't know about you, but there have been times when I've been physically, spiritually, and emotionally exhausted by the number of hats I was wearing versus the crown I was meant to wear.

Many times, women lose their way because there are so many voices trying to tell us who we should be, how we should act, or what we should do. Sometimes those voices are so loud we can't hear anything but their roar. One of the most profound changes in my life has come in learning to listen to the only voice I know I can trust. My good friend Lisa, at Lisa Ingram Ministries, who is anointed in this area, has taught me the power of what it means to meet the Father face to face and receive clear direction. When we go to the King's table, we are picking up our final piece of the armor for battle as we gather messages on our kingdom's behalf in our role as the Holy Spirit.

For years, women have chosen to sit at the world's kitchen table instead of God's banquet table trying to be all things to all people.

Growing and learning to hear your Father's voice, as you sit at his table comes through consistent practice not only in making your needs known but sitting still and listening to what the King has to say in response. For far too long, the Serpents of the world have been telling us our purpose as women. Our place of destiny is much easier and more peaceful than being exhausted and burned out from trying to be wonder woman. All we really have to be is the one thing our Father calls us to be and our husbands desperately need us to become. We are called to be the queen at the banquet table.

In looking more closely at the example of the Proverbs 31 wife, we can find peace. Despite all the amazing, powerful, spectacular things she did, the only thing that she is praised for is what she did for the king by her side.

And she brings him good, not harm, all the days of her life. Proverbs 31:12

It's taken reaching the end of myself, on this fifteen-year journey through the wilderness, for God to get my attention, so he could reveal my real purpose. If I'm seeking first to bring good to my husband all the days of my life, all my other responsibilities and callings fall into place in their natural order.

How does this story end?

God did relocate us out of the wasteland and into a promised land of sorts. He provided us with a *palace* we could never afford through a circumstance too remarkable to explain. The story could fill the pages of another book. I still question some days why he would choose to do such a miraculous thing. I'm learning to embrace that my Heavenly Father is the King, and he loves me that much. Maybe he brought us to this place of peace to finish our books, allowing us to share our story in hopes of helping you realize God wants to bless you with yours. He wants to bless you beyond your imagination if you will only choose to be the queen of nobility he's calling you to be.

From his abundance we have all received one gracious blessing after another. John 1:16 (NLT)

It suddenly became clear as we settled into our new palace, that I'd spent way too much time throughout this journey trying to figure out what God was doing instead of helping my knight in shining armor realize what God had created him to become. God reminded me when we began this trek that he had said this would be an *Abraham and Sarah* journey. When they let go of everything they had, going wherever God said go, they were blessed beyond measure and became the parents of an entire nation. Their descendants walked into a promised land that only God could provide. He can do the same for us if we accept our appointment at the table of prayer which is the pathway to our own *Promised Land*.

We become the queen that our Father desires us to be when we take our chair at His heavenly table and use our position to bring the kingdom into order. Our knightly prince receives the stamp of approval, draped in a robe of righteousness, as we help place the signet ring of leadership on our husband's hand. By God's design, we have the power to usher in peace and destroy the enemy, just as Esther did. Let's roll up our sleeves, fall on our knees, and pray for our husband's hopes, dreams, and destinations. When we do, we straighten our crown, capture his heart, and discover our happily ever after. This is the divine appointment of the queen!

CROWNING POINTS

- Just like Esther we can play a part in saving our family
- There is no greater honor than sitting at the table of the King
- We don't have to fear approaching the throne due to the cross
- God extended his son on the cross as an invitation to come
- Living in nobility is bringing good to our king all the days of his life!

The Nobility Principle

I will straighten my crown!
I will rule like the noble queen God has created me to be.
I WILL...

N o longer allow "ME" to be a victim to the enemy, others, or myself.

O penly communicate in love or step away if necessary.

B elieve I am the royalty that God says that I am.

I dentify my weaknesses, confess them honestly, and let God strengthen them.

L ive intentionally for His kingdom and not my own.

I nvest in the lives of others for the sake of the next generation

T ell others what He has done for me & teach His word to those who do not know Him.

Y earn for His presence and pursue nobility daily.

Appendix A—
Prayer for Soul Ties

Ask forgiveness

Dear God,

I come to you asking for your forgiveness for anyone I have hurt. Have mercy on me for all the things I have done that have caused others pain and heartache. I ask that you heal their pain, remove their hurt, and fill their void. Please forgive me for any words that I have spoken against others, things I have done to others, and grudges I have held against others. I release them into your care to provide perfect healing for the wrongs I have done.

Just as I have wounded others, I ask your help in allowing me to forgive those who have hurt me. Your Word tells me not to take offense, and I lay my pain at your feet for healing and restoration. Right now, I choose to forgive (name each individual you need to forgive) for (name all offenses they have done against you). I love you Lord and release every hurt and pain into your care. You are Jehovah Rapha, the God who heals. By your stripes I am healed, through your blood you have forgiven me, and through your blood I forgive them.

In Jesus' name, Amen.

Break Soul Ties

Dear God,

Your word commands me to be holy and set apart for your purposes and plans. I should not yoke myself to anything or anyone that pulls me away from you. There are many soul connections that I need to break to walk out your perfect plan for my life. I need your power and courage to break any ties I have formed that have attached to my soul, weighed me down, and prevented me from becoming everything you created me to be. James 1:5 says,

If any of you lacks wisdom, you should ask. You give generously to all without finding fault.

I need your wisdom right now to identify every person or thing attached to my soul and break it off according to your will. Help me break every soul tie that has bound me and heal me from all the damage that has been done. I break the soul tie with (name each individual or thing) because of (each sin that was committed that caused the soul tie). I hold up the shield of my faith against all ungodly connections. With the sword of your Word, I sever all strongholds, soul ties, and chains in the physical, emotional, mental, and spiritual realms. They will not bind me or hold me from this day forward. It is finished. Thank you for the cleansing power of the blood of Jesus,

In Jesus' name I pray, Amen.

APPENDIX B

Scripture quotations taken from the King James Version (KJV) – *public domain*

Scripture quotations taken from the English Standard Version (ESV) – public domain.

Scripture quotations taken from GOD'S WORD® (GWT), © 1995 God's Word to the Nations. Used by permission of Baker Publishing Group.

Scripture quotations taken from The Message (MSG). Copyright © 1993, 1994, 1995, 1996, 2000, 2001, 2002. Used by permission of NavPress Publishing Group. Used by permission. All rights reserved.

Scripture quotations taken from the New American Standard Bible (NASB), Copyright © 1960, 1962, 1963, 1968, 1971, 1972, 1973, 1975, 1977, 1995 by The Lockman Foundation. Used by permission.

Scripture quotations taken from the New King James Version (NKJV). Copyright © 1982 by Thomas Nelson, Inc. Used by permission

Scripture quotations taken from the New Living Translation (NLT). Holy Bible, New Living Translation, copyright © 1996, 2004, 2007, 2013, 2015 by Tyndale House Foundation. Used by permission of Tyndale House Publishers Inc., Carol Stream, Illinois 60188. All rights reserved.

ENDNOTES

1   Berlin, Adele. "Abigail: Bible." Jewish Womens Archive. Accessed May 2, 2020. https://jwa.org/encyclopedia/article/abigail-bible.
2   "Home." Focus on the Family, May 1, 2020. https://www.focuson-thefamily.com/. Search *Pornography*
    Arterburn, Stephen. "Every Mans Battle: Winning the War on Sexual Temptation One Victory at a Time." Amazon. WaterBrook, 2020. https://www.amazon.com/Every-Mans-Battle-Winning-Temptation/dp/1578563682.
3   "Homepage." Homepage. Accessed May 2, 2020. https://jentezen-franklin.org/. Search *Fasting*
4   Durden-Smith, Jo, and Diane DeSimone. Sex and the Brain. New York: Warner Books, 1984
5   Moore, Beth. "Esther: It's Tough Being a Woman." Amazon. LifeWay Press, 2008. https://www.amazon.com/Esther-Its-Tough-Being-Woman/dp/1415865965.

ACKNOWLEDGEMENTS

Dedicated to all the people who believed in the message we wanted to share. We would not have had the courage to step forward and write this book without your support.

To my husband, the king by my side, who has stood by me for thirty plus years as my partner and best friend. Together we have forged the lessons and stories of our own journey in this book with the passion to do our part to battle for this beautiful thing called marriage. Thank you "for better or worse, and for richer and poorer." You are my knight in shining armor. I love you forever!

Thanks to our children for their support and encouragement throughout this journey:

Jordan, thanks for your immeasurable help in graphic design, consulting, managing our social media, and challenging us to reach your generation to save marriages.

Rachel, thanks for sharing your artistic eye with us, designing our e-book covers, shooting our photos to capture our best look and for being honest about your ideas on this endeavor when we couldn't see where to go next.

John David, thanks for your patience at times when we had to work long hours and your willingness to do the hard things on days when it was really busy.

Most importantly thanks to my Abba Father "who is able to do immeasurably more than all we ask or imagine, according to His power that is at work within us". Ephesians 3:20

ABOUT THE AUTHORS

Dan and Lydia White are recognized leaders in single, married, and family relationships. They are award winning authors, admired teachers, and sought-after speakers. They are the founders of *Living In Nobility*, a ministry dedicated to helping individuals live out their divine purpose and understand their true identity as a child of the King. Together, they've helped countless couples put their lives back in order. Dan is an ordained minister and holds a MA in Ministry. Lydia has a MA in Ministry with a concentration in pastoral counseling. They co-authored *Chaos in the Castle or Peace in the Palace,* a companion book for wives. Celebrating over 30 years of marriage and having successfully raised three children, they empower couples to live in nobility as rulers over their kingdom, marriage, and family.

Your Next Steps to Becoming a Noble Queen

⚜ TAKE THE FREE ASSESSMENT
Discover your rating on the chaos or peace spectrum

⚜ DOWNLOAD THE FREE PALACE PLAN
Every woman's guide to happily ever after

⚜ STRENGTHEN YOUR MARRIAGE AND FAMILY
Resources for capturing your warrior's heart and possessing your peaceful palace

⚜ ACCESS TOOLS FOR SMALL GROUPS
For leaders of Women's and Couple's Small Groups, we have questions and exercises to create conversation and spiritual growth. Note: The Companion book, *Marriage Warrior* for husbands can be purchased online.

For these downloads and much more:
www.ChaosOrPeace.us

COMPANION RESOURCE

If you enjoyed *Chaos in the Castle or Peace in the Palace*, empower your husband to lead with nobility and fight for your marriage and win or transform your couples small group with:

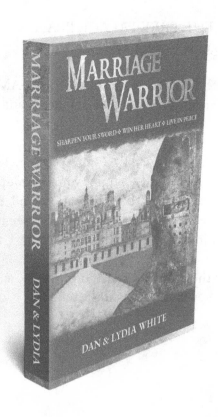